A Phenomena-Based Physics

Sound ~ Light ~ Heat

Volume 1 of 3
for

Grade 6

Manfred von Mackensen

Waldorf
PUBLICATIONS
RESEARCH INSTITUTE FOR Waldorf EDUCATION

Sound ~ Light ~ Heat

Electricity, Magnetism & Electromagnetism,
Mechanics, Hydraulics and Aerodynamics
as Subjects in an
Introductory Physics
6th through 8th Grades

Volume 1 of 3
for

Grade 6

by
Manfred von Mackensen
Pedagogical Research Department
Union of German Waldorf Schools
Kassel, West Germany, 1992

translated and edited by John H. Petering
August 1994

Printed with support from the Waldorf Curriculum Fund

Published by:
Waldorf Publications at the
Research Institute for Waldorf Education
38 Main Street
Chatham, NY 12037

Title: *A Phenomena-Based Physics: Sound, Light, Heat: Grade 6*
Author: Manfred von Mackensen
Editors: David Mitchell and John Petering
Translation: John Petering

German original copyright 1987, 1992 by Manfred von Mackensen,
Kassel, West Germany
First printing © 1994 by AWSNA Publications

Revised edition © 2017
ISBN #978-1-943582-21-1
Layout: Ann Erwin
Proofreader: Melissa Merkling
Cover: Moon shadows on the beach during solar eclipse
August 22, 2017, eastern United States

Table of Contents

Contents

Introduction

I. PREFACE

The following chapters describe a selected area of teaching—physics—the contents, initial thoughts, yes even the entire construction of the teaching material and many teaching methods, all drawn from the treasure chest of Waldorf pedagogy. But, simply by working through the descriptions for an *individual* physics topic given here, someone foreign to the Waldorf methodology can hardly achieve intimacy with the whole of this pedagogy. And yet, it is only from this whole that such particulars (e.g., the physics lessons) can arise or be available.

What is presented here can be only a kind of *indication* of this whole, that at first stands open and unknown. At the same time, this material *can* serve as a stimulus also for the teaching efforts of those not familiar with Waldorf education. The present material could even be useful from a variety of viewpoints, e.g., finding little-known physics experiments.

Still, in spite of these obstacles, the fundamental concepts of the Waldorf approach to natural science should reach a wider audience. Certainly, it will be in the spirit of the *preconceptions of the author* and the working-group here in Kassel (the basis for this whole project), including their understanding about scientific theories, developmental psychology and commercial starting points—insofar as an introduction can draw comparisons to contemporary ideas.

Although this book alone is not really an introduction to the essentials of Waldorf pedagogy, nor can it even fully develop a scientific foundation for our approach, yet we must attempt to highlight our preliminary understanding, which has been used effectively, and draw attention to it in the context of the contemporary science education literature. The starting points of our work should be made visible; thereby, skeptical readers will be able to select something useful, try it out, and perhaps have it make sense sooner than later.

Whoever is new to this subject, or initially wants to spare themselves a discussion of foundational scientific theory and educational psychology (possibly many readers), could perhaps read only the final section of this introductory chapter: "VII. To the Teacher," which summarizes many theoretical and practical points. After that, they could experiment with the various lesson outlines of a phenomena-based approach to physics. Thus, they will have the necessary examples in front of them, and later may go back to read the rest of the background to this approach to studying the sciences, especially physics.

[Note: The following sections have been summarized from von Mackensen's detailed discussion, since most of the educational and philosophical authors cited are not well-known in the English-speaking countries. For a full critique of the philosophical underpinnings presented by Dr. Mackensen, a full translation of his introduction is available from the Waldorf Publications clearinghouse upon request, at no cost.]

II. TEACHING, TECHNOLOGY & LIFE

Basically, we have less and less success guiding young people in learning and work, both at school and at home. Education slips away from this generation; although the amount of scientific work given to them is greater than ever before! Elaborate reforms, allocation of financial resources and dedicated administration in the schools have not helped the whole. Plainly, neither the analytical, technical, nor legal modes of thinking truly relate to those deeper aspects of the human being capable of transformation and learning. The human forces which allow people to form their spirituality, enliven their soul, and enable them to grow, plainly lie in another realm from the modern scientific way of thinking.

Educational writers themselves point to a need for a reorientation of science teaching to make it relevant to people's daily life, in view of the "lack of impact of a technically-oriented science teaching, which tries to tackle the teaching and learning process using the [quantitative] methods invented by that same science...." (Duit 1981) The fact that schools aren't easily reformable with technocratic means is due to the fact that "the first phase of reform was ... too foreign from the children, went off into abstract scientific criteria. ... Along with a structurally-rooted, growing unemployment, the principle of competition shifts down into ever lower grades. And, as schools allow such selective and competitive modes to creep in, it only increases the impoverishment of students in terms of social experiences, emotional connections, and feeling-filled learning possibilities.

"On the heels of the discovery of possibilities for early learning came performance-based teaching programs, minutely planned class periods (with well-planned teaching behavior, and expected student behavior), and increased *demands for more content* and more technical-professional scientific topics in the lessons. To our dismay today, we actually *establish the isolation and alienation of the human being.*" (Silkenbeumer 1981) Perhaps we can explore further this contrast between the bright well-defined world of science with the dark, less consciously understood world of life, albeit in a living manner, using open-ended characterizations, and always mindful of the whole range of human activity.

Another description of how these two principles from the world of life and of science infiltrate everything is given in the last great letters of Erich Fromm. He characterizes them as "having" and "being": "Indeed, to one for whom having is the main form of relatedness to the world, ideas that can not easily be pinned down (penned down) are frightening—like everything else that grows, changes, and thus is not controllable." (Fromm 1976) After showing how the current crises of humanity spring from the ideology of fixation and having, Fromm describes how the modern technological world promotes a marketing-character, people who "experience themselves as a commodity ... whose success depends largely on how well they sell themselves on the market" and, dedicated to pursuing the quantitative side of life, become *estranged* from their living surroundings and from their own self. "Most striking, at first glance, is that Man has made himself into a god because he has acquired the technical capacity for a second creation of the world, replacing the first creation by the God of traditional religion. ... Human beings, in the state of their greatest real impotence, in connection with science and technology *imagine* themselves to be *omnipotent*." (Fromm 1976a)

If we shy away from Fromm's pedagogical indications, we can still value his observations and views and note again that *it matters for the whole of humanity, for everyone.* So, whether it admits it or not, education also is tensioned between these poles of "having" and "being," or between convergent and divergent issues. (Schumacher 1979)

Convergent issues are of a type which *can* be dealt with and converge on a stable solution simply by applying more time, intelligence, or resources (even without higher forces of life, a wider consciousness, or personal experience). Dealing with *divergent* problems with more study only produces more polarity—they require a higher level of being, beyond mere logic, where the seeming opposition of polarities can be transcended. A classic example is finding the right educational methods, where the right formula or answer is seemingly never found in the opposing ideas of more form vs. more autonomy. Divergent issues involve a higher realm, including both freedom and direct inner experience.

We all must cope with our scientific world; its development is necessary for a free consciousness. But now it challenges us to find its limits so that the living environment, society, and the human spirit can breathe. **This problem is truly the deepest, most global problem of our time.** Within science, challenges lead us to new *scientific theories,* and many, diverse initiatives exist, but with only meager results up to now. (We will indicate our relation to each of these initiatives below.) When our thinking within the living world is challenged, it can lead to *Goetheanism*, to a phenomenology rich in living ideas. But, mere concerns in the living world lead only to mythology.

III. THE LANDSCAPE OF SCIENCE

PRESUMED CERTAINTY VS. LIFE

In recent years there have been many articles published that discuss the philosophy of science (How do we know the world?). Science teachers adopt the same well-accepted, positivistic habits of thought as more technical writers, presuming that conventional quantitative methods do give us a real knowledge of nature. Yet, if we delve more deeply into what many writers in the philosophy of science say about this, what emerges is not at all so cut and dried—nor clear. The fundamental question is: What is the relationship between our selves and the world out there? This is one of *the* fundamental questions of philosophy. Many philosophers such as Descartes, Kant and Goethe have wrestled with the question. Does my mind (soul, spirit) have any real connection with my body (the world of matter)?

Even contemporary educators acknowledge the subtleties of this relationship: "What scientific research achieves, in the best case, is not a plain portrayal of reality. The theory of science has shown that the researcher is not only interwoven with his experiments and the measuring apparatus he uses, but also (in a much more subtle but potent way) is intermeshed with his whole theoretical and mental framework, with his very concepts and way of questioning, with his definitions and hypotheses."[1] (Wieland 1981) And in 20th century physics itself, exact results have come about which do not illuminate a clear reality, and indeed never can. The Copenhagen Interpretation about quantum theory (1926) early on led a leading physicist to say "… the reality is different, it depends on whether we observe or not … and we must remember that what we observe is not Nature itself, but nature *as expressed to our manner of questioning.*" (Heisenberg 1959; see also K.F. von Weizsäcker 1971)

This awareness, beginning first in physics, now spreading to many other fields, forces us to recognize that our relation to the world is not as simple as we might have thought. Although there are myriad ways of considering nature, for *our* path the image of nature we develop fully develops and ripens only *through the human being*—the human being is not superfluous. Our preconceptions (what T. Kuhn calls our paradigm or framework of what we take "world" to be) matter a lot—they condition the very character of what we come up with. If we really think about it, the very reality which science presumes cannot be thought about as something real "out there," with our selves as something separate, a kind of onlooker; rather its reality consists in our mutual relationship and intimate connections with the world.

THE SOLE AUTHORITY?

While it's true that the conventional literature doesn't claim to be the only valid method, at least not *explicitly,* still, this attitude is *implemented,* in that empirical or positivistic habits are accepted and implicit in the way science and teaching are pursued. Actually, some educators have come very close to touching on these questions, and their ideas are significant not because they pose a particular problem, but because they discuss *standards* of what is "good" science.

They usually presume that our knowledge and theories relate to a pre-existing objectively material world. And "what gives [this method] certainty is a clearly marked path back to the evidence of data." (Jung 1982) This presumes an aspect of phenomena separate from our conceptualizing, which is part of an objective world, existing *before* we think about the phenomena. So "reality" must consist in a *collection of basic phenomena* (i.e., all our perceptions in the living world) which is accessible to all persons.

So the fundamental question becomes: Is there some sort of pre-existing objectively material world "out there" and our observations lead us "in here" (in my mind) to think about it and formulate theories and understanding? Are "phenomena" *something* independent of me, pre-existing, or are phenomena actually my experience of a relationship between self and world, awakening and coming to light in the perceiving, beholding human being? This is a very tricky, subtle but *very* important question.

STRENGTHS OF MODERN SCIENCE

On the other hand, in a pragmatic view, people set aside the questions of whether the knowledge is "real," and presume the task of natural science is to simply reproduce an image of this layer of reality as precisely as possible, and organize it in a comprehensible way. So, even if a subjective prior conception and historically-related world paradigm play a role, then the image we build up (modern natural science) would have the following strengths:

- The path from theory back to phenomena can be clearly retraced using understandable concepts, as must be since this method deals only with the aspect of phenomena understandable in thinkable, quantitative categories. Thus, this whole construct will be *comprehensible.*
- As we go beyond mere acceptance of an invention and mere application to build up theories of immense breadth at the highest level, daring and bold intuition plays a role. Such ideas open unbounded possibilities of activity and schooling to the human intellect. Thus, the whole is *inspiring.*
- In applying such theories and methods in working with nature, technology arises; we needn't argue its effectiveness. Such a science is *usable.*

Even if the whole range of scientific theories isn't taken as objective general truth, nevertheless most people feel that, in fact, it *does* achieve the best that could be achieved *by* and *for* people, with the means at their disposal. Although it might encompass and weave in more of reality with ever better revisions of its theories, they can't see how anyone could achieve something more understandable, more inspiring, or more effective! Most people concede such a natural science may not be the only one possible, but believe it is the best that can be achieved, and thus should be acknowledged and supported by everyone.

PURE PERCEPTION, A WELL WITHOUT A PIPE

We have explored the conventional ideas in order to contrast our approach of phenomenology or Goetheanism. Our starting point for all knowledge and thinking is actually *perception* through the senses, the active participation and perception through human senses of a living human body. But pure perception is very elusive; we can't actually *say* anything about the senses unless we go beyond pure sensing. We can explore the world by means of perceptions, but we can't discuss the world in perceptions. Nevertheless, we start with perception as a relationship, one that goes far deeper than these concepts we are using to discuss it, and even lies *prior* to them.

But, we can't prove this, since proof already goes beyond perception to use conceptualization. We can have pure perception only when we *hold back* our capacity for forming ideas and concepts. (Steiner 1918) **Only pure perception exists per se—but we cannot say anything about it.** The reality of the way it arises in the human soul is actually something holy; what we could say about the content of perception is it is a human product, always a prior conception and a theory conditioned by the living world.

THINKING REVIVES IN PERCEPTION

A person could object: Then every theory is just arbitrary; but if they are neatly formulated, they relate to the world because they are technically usable. We respond: True. Concepts and theories are certainly added to perception by *human* effort, however they plainly prove to belong to the world if people have made an effort, but correspond to experiences of *a different* side of the world, one not revealed in perceptions. Our thinking is an essential complement to pure perception. In thinking, people have a kind of organ for this other side of the world, which is most active when we reflect on the world of senses rather than the world of thoughts. Goethe, in contrast to many modern thinkers, understood perceiving as a particular conceptual activity.

PARADIGMS AND THE LIVING WORLD

As soon as one transcends this reductionist way of asking questions, and thoughtfully begins to work with the qualitative side of human experience, there is no longer such a thing as phenomena *independent* of theory (conceptually organized perceptions). The phenomena are the aspects of the world we live in through being conscious in perception. In the process of thinking, through a balanced consciousness, out of the experience of perceiving naturally unfolds a definite kind of conceptual activity. The more we live in the perceiving side of this balance, the more the true being of the world will actually speak in the thoughts and concepts which the phenomena lead us to form. Pure perception exists per se; phenomena are already passing over to a more conceptual side.

This is important because the implications are very broad and deep. The reductionist approach, considering mind and self as separate from the world out there, has a split implicit in it: "The spiritual and moral ... dealt with as epi-phenomena. ... On the one side is human life with its values and choices, on the other, a scientific Utopia: Man as Machine." (Jung 1981c)

INDIVIDUAL DECISIONS

Since we can prove neither method with logic alone, it must remain a free decision of each person which way they wish to understand their relation to the world: theories about the world which allow one to manipulate the world, or a relationship of perceiving. Basically, we can only say that the author has worked through the phenomena in this way, and *intends* to work with them thus. The Western tradition tends toward manipulation of the nature out there; a complementary approach lives more richly in the phenomena and uses more the subjective, qualitative side of perceiving. It does require a carefully schooled, balanced, thoughtful consideration of the phenomena and of our process of forming concepts.

IV. ALTERNATIVE SCIENCE – NO THANKS?

LONGING AND HORROR

We have reached the most explosive place in our introductory discussion. Even in one of the most inviting works on teaching methods, it can happen that when it comes to the theme of alternative approaches to science, the whole style changes dramatically: Irony, dire predictions and all-out polemics surface. This *although* or perhaps *just because* alternative science increasingly becomes the vague object of longing of many people.

The editor of *Chemistry and Technology News* proposes, "Do you believe that it would be possible ... to develop a rational scientific method which doesn't pursue just this reductionist approach to nature, rather a method which sees as much of the whole and simultaneously isn't useful technically? You say yourself that's a royal task. ... Couldn't we at least strengthen a consciousness that there exists a natural-scientific-technical world conception other than our own? Are there certain sciences which are not intended for utility, but earlier on proceed in a phenomenological way, and if there are, shouldn't we pursue them?" There is nothing to say but YES!

Another author expresses alarm that "science is not features of rationality or freedom, not basics of education; it is a commodity. The scientist himself becomes a salesman for this merchandise, they are not judges about truth and falsehood. ... The starting point is not truth, or the newest level of science, or some other empty generality; the starting point is the equivalence of all traditions." (Feyerabend 1981)

The anti-science effect, which has grown so strong today, arises not only because of ecological, political-social crises, but is due to a split in the living stratum of the soul into calculable scientific concepts on one layer and feelings and moral (or animal) impulses on another, which directs practical dealings in life, and yet becomes ever more isolated. It is also on the rise since people no longer hesitate to speak about this split out of "respect" for the acknowledged science.

HUMAN POWERS

In the last centuries the scientific view of nature has established only what the Cartesian revolution, the methods of Galileo, Newton, etc., contain: a kind of imperialistic knowledge which serves the orientation of the human being toward control of the cosmos. The reason the causal-analytic approach to natural science requires an alternative is not because it provides too little *information* about the world, but rather because it doesn't activate our soul-spiritual forces.

WEAKNESSES OF PHENOMENOLOGY

According to the above ideas, there are three things phenomenology cannot have: It is not understandable in laymen's terms (in concepts which are definable in a mechanical framework); it has not progressed very far nor inwardly developed (doesn't have 400 years behind it); it is not usable in a naïvely unconscious way, in a mechanical sense, without a look-back at the whole situation in nature.

The most negative is a lack of external provability, without a mechanistic mode of thinking. This is unavoidable, since this provability arises from just those conceptual tools which now should be extended and complemented, namely the quantitative approach, and ultimately mathematics.

EXTENSION OF BOTH METHODS: PROPADEUTICS (LIBERAL-ARTS INSTRUCTION)

Alternative and rule-based science complement each other, and neither possesses all the necessary aspects for education; we can dispense with neither one. Even where we can explore with a quantitative approach, we must go inward.

For example, in the gas laws, if we wish to really penetrate the matter, we must go inside the mere formula $V_t = V_0 (1 + 1/273 \, t)$. As the heating is increased, the increased tension in the gas container (pressure) is experienced as a reflection of the activity of heat and the increase in measurable volume.

Analytical thinking initially creates distance; but then, an inner connection with the processes in the world, insofar as the magnitudes in the formula we work out are inwardly felt and experienced. Such a going inward is the starting point of all phenomenological research.

If the advanced technical material presented at the introductory level of a broad, liberal-arts curriculum should be limited, what should be correspondingly expanded? This leads us to a human basis for a new teaching method: basing the themes on the development of the student. The questions then become: In which grade should physics start? What ideas should it pursue?

V. DEVELOPMENTAL PSYCHOLOGY:
TRADITIONAL DIVISION OF PHYSICS-MATERIAL

In the pedagogical works of Rudolf Steiner there are many places where he points to the essential reorientation of the lessons at the onset of pre-puberty. He indicates how, mainly after 11²/3 year (6th grade), the young person separates out the living and ensouled from the dead aspect in the surroundings and is now able to recognize it. Therefore, we can be attentive to this moment, understand why the study of mineralogy and physics can begin then, and relate to the young person's developing natural interest in life.

CURRICULUM OVERVIEW

In 6th grade—when the physics studies begin—the way of regarding things is still phenomenological and imagistic in all the topics. It is not yet abstracted in the sense, for example, of deriving general Laws of Nature. The material-causal method of school physics is kept out. However, in the **7th grade** this comparative-imagistic approach already receives a new direction. Certainly not toward scientific models, atoms and the like, but rather toward work, livelihood, trade connections, and thereby to technical applications in life. Since young people will at puberty begin to distance themselves from their parental home, they are occupied with the question: How can a person help himself along in the world through clear ideas? And, underlying this: How can a person contribute something of value in the outer world of work?

At the end of the 7th grade physics studies, *as* an essentially technical topic, we present the mechanical theories involved with the use of levers. Simple experiments, scientific systematics and a technical-practical understanding of the apparatus all occur together in mechanics. Out of such a treatment, we reach the starting point of classical physics. However, a systematic treatment of the other topics in physics founded on this does not quite follow yet. Even in **8th grade**, we will use quantitative or expressible formulas only in particular cases—for example, in the treatment of current in a circuit or in the pressure calculations for fluid mechanics of air or water—but they will still be connected with direct observations in the classroom.

In 9th grade after the material-causal explanations of the telephone and locomotive have been treated thoroughly (for example, with current-time diagrams, vapor-pressure curves and thermal mass comparisons), this phenomena-based method arrives at a quantitative systematics for the first time only in the **10th grade.** There, even while quantitative, the view shifts back to the human being: How we predict through calculations of a parabolic trajectory is now thoughtfully considered as a phenomenon of knowledge. And, only after the question of perception and reality in the "supra-sensible" is worked through in the **11th grade** via the study of modern electrical inventions (Tesla coil, Roentgen rays, radioactivity), do the light and color studies of the block in **12th grade** penetrate again to a Goetheanism. However, the methodology [and epistemology] is now clear to the students.

So, moving toward the 9th grade, the curriculum increasingly lays aside the phenomenological approach, as we increasingly lay aside nature. With the analytical method and use of technical instruments, a non-spiritual, material causality chain now becomes the goal of the lessons. This is what is appropriate here and therefore—pedagogically viewed—nonetheless a Goethean method (Goetheanism in the consideration of a thought sequence). From these technical-practical topics of the 8th and 9th grades and their social implications, we turn around again in the 10th grade and focus on the thinking human being. The process by which we develop knowledge and the relationship it has thereby to the world is raised to the phenomenon here. Through such a careful and interconnected arrangement of steps in physics, the young students gradually awake to an exploration of their own methods of knowing—and that is the real question.

SUMMARY

The so-called abstract study of natural science, using causal-analytical methods, actually lies near other paths. (see chart next page) First we can consider the overall experience reading downward in the central column: A restriction to increasing abstraction and models, providing the all-permeating meaning of the world, and degrading the initial holistic experience to a misleading reflex, a byproduct of the model (an illusion). Knowledge becomes imprisoned in the lower circle, and people run around in a senseless experience of a causal-analytic mechanistic world. They develop gigantic technical works and enjoy everything that they love.

In contrast, working upward on the right is a deepening of a phenomenological way of considering the world, leading people to truly grasp who they are, and thereby building a basis for a new approach to the spirit—a holistic experience. They enjoy what they *realize*. With this we note how the 6th grade begins with holistic knowledge; the 9th grade moves to causal-analytic thinking but not yet models; and mechanical thought in 10th, where we stop.

TWO PATHS OF NATURAL SCIENCE CONTRASTED

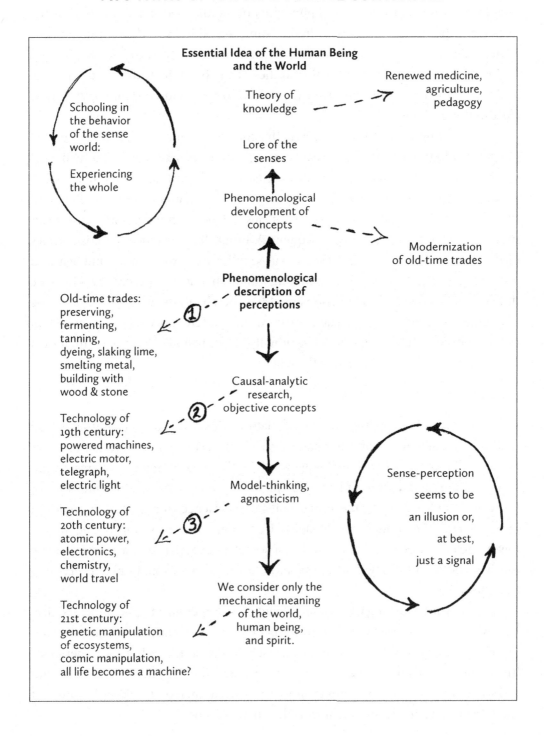

VI. PEDAGOGICAL METHODS

Nowadays, natural science is pursued with the goal of bringing facts to light and utilizing them technically. Whether research makes an impression on the public depends on the usefulness of these facts and on what can be produced from them. The analytical method is impressive and shows the basic significance of the things investigated. But, how do things stand with knowing?

In order to unify and order the innumerable facts, physicists build theories and conceptual models, e.g., the wave model of light. They know, in principle, that every model has limitations and that above all there are always phenomena which will contradict it. A model applies only to certain phenomena; for others, one must construct a contrasting model for the same topic. So it is that, admittedly, no knowledge of the whole arises. Nevertheless, scientific models such as the light theories or the atom-concept (which never touch the essence of the matter) are commonly viewed as the essence, or at least as steps to the essentials—as much in the popular view as in scientific consciousness. In thinking this we overlook the fact that questions about "essence" fall entirely outside the categories of physics, cannot be included in them, and equally cannot be answered by them. Nevertheless, to the student every model is naturally taken as an answer to essential questions, a statement about the ground of existence, although the students are not consciously asking about it! The narrowness of these kinds of answers cannot really be appreciated by the student, since s/he does not yet comprehend the role played by pure thinking in forming world-conceptions, or the way a free activity of the human being is connected with it. The student is oriented more to perception.

Abstract conceptions, however, which do not originate from the phenomena, become misconceptions: as if not invented by us, but rather as coarsely material or also as magical beings which we light upon and then believe that they stand as final cause behind everything there is. And so the phenomena give rise to an ontological misunderstanding of physics[2] [misunderstanding the nature of being or reality].

Goethe's natural-scientific work, as set forth by Rudolf Steiner, developed a little-known qualitative way of observing nature and now is constantly producing and extending a literature of Goetheanism and phenomenology. This concrete path built around an intercourse with qualities of perception will actually bring the perceiving human being to reality. Due to the style of teaching typical of the later elementary years, there is a fundamental need for qualitative natural-scientific methods, since only these make an attempt to work in accord with the essentials, to work on just those questions deeply experienced at this stage of life. The question of whether such an approach promotes complete understanding can remain open, but certainly it is more complete than that promoted by models. For us, the pedagogical value of the teacher's striving and his inner, spiritual activity exceeds the value of mere knowing.

TWO PATHS TO NATURE

This suggests two methods of conceiving nature (and thereby also the world) which at first are unconnected, namely: (1) the material-causal method, which wants to find a model of the ultimate cause through analyzing matter, which is thought to lie at the foundation, and (2) the Goethean method of phenomenology, which seeks to order rich perceptions of nature as a totality. These two ways of approaching nature are both contained in Dr. Steiner's curriculum. However, he didn't intermix them, nor did he present them interspersed with one another. Rather, we find them organized into the curriculum with the analytical following the phenomenological—the aim being to place them in an evaluable contrast by the 12th grade.

VII. TO THE TEACHER

HEALTHY AND UNHEALTHY PREPARATION

This book has been written precisely for those who won't receive it first: the students. Teachers will doubtless receive it, perhaps with a sigh of relief. It may seem that in it lies a wealth of physics material, neatly packaged and awaiting use like pre-assembled concepts, stashed away in a deep freeze. The impression that I have carefully tried to create, to be understood perhaps only later, is that such a hope cannot be realized through a book; and if it could it should be forbidden! The students do not live off the stuff from a book, but from the initiative of the teachers and from their spiritual wrestling and persistence to blaze a path for them on how to see the world. As the teacher learns, so the students learn. Whoever is in good command of the subject—knowing that she must not only freshly order things but must unlock new sides of it *for herself)*—will be able to teach out of direct, spiritual experience—she will inwardly reach the class. In order for the physics covered here to encompass this dimension, it was necessary on the one hand to make the subject easy for the teacher, so it could be expressed in words, and on the other hand, also necessary to make it hard for the teacher. This challenge comes from me, since I can understand the full scope of the material only in certain scientific and pedagogical terms.

Following Goethe's beginnings and in the spirit of Dr. Steiner's theory of knowledge, a person should *attend to nature's phenomena and simultaneously attend to the inner activity and experiences of the [perceiving] human being;* then the person must attempt to break free of the rigid [mental] labels of "particles," "waves" and "energies." New, basic ideas are of great value to go more deeply into nature, but these are radically different from the traditional concepts of school physics, and from a materially disposed, conventional understanding.

My ideal would be to set aside the quick definitions in phoronomic terms [purely mechanical motion], and lead everything over into open, seemingly indeterminate concepts. What light "is," what sound is "in actuality," what is "the basis" of heat—all this cannot be clarified without further ado, but must be achieved by experienced observations and thinking on the part of the teacher and the students. We call upon the reader's own perceptive judgment. (Compare Goethe's concept: *Anschauende Urteilskraft,* "perceptive power of beholding.")

Clearly physics classes shouldn't be merely a list of points out of the great book of scientific authority, but should be spontaneous, without limits at the outset to questions involving only quantifiable measurements. Naturally, this requires a lot, namely: **an alternative way of thinking,** the greatest possible individual sense of orientation, and **a familiarity with the phenomena.** Only to the extent that this text seeks to pursue such difficult goals, should it be allowed to appear. An easy, practical collection of obvious school-knowledge—provided it is good—is only a help to the teacher who is already in desperate straits; however, it undervalues just these deeper needs of the students.

Aside from aiding such a direct, untrammeled, personal spiritual quest for knowledge, teaching has, naturally, a more ordinary side: We also must furnish the students with actual knowledge of the thinking and the day-to-day business of our technological civilization. For this the teacher needs information which is refined and prepared. So I have interwoven a few such indications in the main text and also provided some related topics. There we can see how we can work without abstract scientific models and hypotheses so far removed from the phenomena.

EXPERIENCES WITH THIS METHOD

Interesting teaching experiences have arisen meanwhile from colleagues who have received this book just because physics was new for them. In the worst cases, the students said "That was, certainly, all very logical," meaning that the phenomena were already clear (they weren't led to previously unknown phenomena). On the one hand, they were caught up too little by the wonder of the world; on the other, not enough difficult questions were given them.

Now, this raises several issues. The students have a point: New facets of the world must be shown in wonder-filled, previously unknown effects. The students like to plunge into manifestations of the lively activity of strange forces, they like to see things which can be conjured forth with simple manipulation. Whenever the teacher surprises them with unexpected phenomena, that makes an impression! The manipulative, perceptible side of the world must come to the fore. True, without a wakeful musing and reflecting over the experiments, a certain superficiality and inconsiderateness would be fostered. Nevertheless, I do a few direct, surprising presentations. But, in caring for the perceptive side of things, one should not neglect the thought-aspect.

To an art of experimentation belongs also an art of conceptualization. A person will place himself perceptively into everyday phenomena and, out of his own careful pondering, form new concepts, so as to build wholly on the phenomena. Then experiments which appear commonplace will no longer seem merely logical but, perceiving with new eyes, will allow the thinking to reach up to the working ideas of nature so they really speak. (see Goethe's essay on plants, regarding his "seeing" the archetypal plant) It shouldn't happen—as it often does in conventional physics—that the teacher simply presents how things are supposed to be seen. Goetheanism as pronouncement remains mere semantics.

Conventional physics, on the one hand, relies on everyday thought-forms which have a life of their own and therefore easily take root in the students. On the other hand, the more the teacher has the foundations of Goetheanism in herself, still utilizing and experiencing it even on days when she doesn't teach it, the more she is able to call it forth out of the simplest phenomena and give it a permanent basis in the students' souls.

Using a book to show the way to do this is, naturally, risky. In the worst situations, the impression could appear that the proposed material is too childish and that the 6th grade material should already have been done in the 5th grade as it lacks causal thinking. By all means, twelve-year-old students (grade 7) should already practice a thinking which takes its stand in the compelling links or relationships between specific phenomena. We only have to try and develop a thinking *freer* than a thinking which explains the appearances out of processes of the matter which is supposed to make up the substratum of reality. This will be shown particularly in the section on light.

UNUSUAL LANGUAGE

It is necessary in the 6th and 7th grades, and somewhat in the 8th, that the students immerse themselves in the qualitative aspect of things. Thereby, their experience receives an orientation toward objectivity, not through analytical abstractions, but in careful expression and in connecting to the phenomena. If one wants to work in this way, one needs *expressions* and *a language* which embraces *the feeling side of experience.* The one-sided cultivation of the cognitive faculties, basically only rational instructional elements and goals only in the cognitive domain, fails to take into account and neglects the feeling and doing side of the human being. The student learns individual pieces of knowledge. But the feelings will not be expressed, developed and differentiated: "The feeling of senseless learning becomes often a feeling of senseless life, the seed of a depressive orientation." (Fischer-Wasels 1977) Through abstract teaching, the desire for an emotional reality can lead to a splitting of personality. As in many such articles, a rigorously restricted subject matter is called for and, for the natural sciences, a strong consideration of the phenomena. [see in the U.S., the move by the PSSC curriculum project to emphasize simple phenomena with simple apparati – Trans.]

As experience shows, such a *restriction* of the science content will be of little help if a *new art of thought*—a *different language* and an experiential way of working connected with the phenomena—does not simultaneously replace a mere taking up of one phenomenon after another. One can only put *something else,* not nothing, in the place of an abstract thinking that has become a scientizing. This "something different" should engage the complete *experience* of the human being, not only our *conceptualizing* faculties. That is to say: In the course content, new fundamental concepts are necessary! The technical language doesn't suffice.

What is attempted in this book is to utilize such language as *unites* the feeling with the conceptual. But, this is the main snag for professionally trained people. Rather than an illumination of actual perceptions, they expect to combine definitions and concepts purified of every experiential aspect (e.g., *phoronomy* or kinematics; motion without regard for the actual units). Already on pedagogical grounds, we cannot here concur with this goal. Thus, we must attempt to intersperse these rational and emotional instructional elements, not only like a spice, but rather to draw them right out of *the things at hand.* From the most fundamental perceptions to the most all-encompassing thoughts, it is important to always speak to the whole human being and to truly look on concrete phenomena of the world right through to the end. That leads necessarily to unconventional, open-ended concepts and indications.

We take into consideration that these new, open-ended fundamental concepts have their source in perceptions saturated with feeling, they lead on to meaningful thoughts, and they have a structure which can be evaluated as a result of their relationship to actual perceptions. We aren't dealing with a complex of feelings arising from some kind of subjective evaluation, but rather with elements of science, [a conscious process]. The full earnestness of the task of physics teaching, as presented herein, will work as a stimulus when one has the insight that the central concepts we strive for aim not at a childish prettying-up of the barren subject matter of nature with all sorts of subjectivity, but rather, our aim is to open up a new scientific reality out of our own personal perceptions—however modest the beginning introduced here might be.

You might notice that the new concepts in the section on light are a bit further developed toward a Goethean phenomenology. With heat, especially in grade 6, such a Goethean approach would be impressive but also becomes more difficult to grasp. Acoustics in grade 6 is also organized around unconventional ideas, and only in the subsequent grades will become more familiar. But in acoustics, these new concepts do not take such an unusual form as in light studies. Electricity and magnetism are presented in a qualitative way and lead to concepts formed in a particular way, though these remain mainly empty forms, as yet unfilled with much that is compelling or germinal. In mechanics, least of all have we made a beginning into an experientially clear treatment of force and pressure (hydromechanics).

We are dealing here with a search for an understanding that takes as its starting point the human being. In order to live into such a new mode of approach, the epistemological orientation must be spoken of in an extensive work, amply supported by philosophical and anthropological points as are here only begun. And the physicist would nevertheless still not be free of a deep uneasiness—for, instead of studying the rewarding scientific developments of this century, we have apparently given them up in favor of a new consideration of Aristotle. Whether this is necessary, something to put up with, or just foolish cannot be determined from concepts but only in one's own intimate meeting with the perceptions.

If I occasionally draw on concepts from the writings of Dr. Steiner, this should provide those familiar with his work a quick means for further reading. However, the seeds of the phenomenological method and what is therefore useful in teaching are not dependent on these references. Thus, I hope also to invite many useful contributions from the non-Waldorf teacher.

THE BOOK'S LAYOUT AND ABBREVIATING THE MATERIAL

Concerning the **structure of this series of three books for grades 6, 7, and 8,** may I say that it follows the sequence of grades 6 through 8. The experimental descriptions are, with some exceptions, extracted from the text and inserted after individual chapters. Appended in Book 3 is a list of equipment and, as a possible deepening, a few supplemental topics.

The extent of material presented often exceeds what can be handled in one block, especially if a teacher is presenting this for the first time and isn't at all familiar with many of the phenomena. However, one should not omit an entire topic, as for example, the one usually coming last: magnetism. At least a central experience from each topic is desired.

In attempting to **shorten** this syllabus, the teacher will have a hard time, as I have attempted to build up each topic carefully and thoroughly out of the simplest phenomena and thus establish a line of thought to foundational ideas. Thereby, a certain systematizing has entered in. Each proposition is prepared for and also proven from the preceding one. Such a structured form is indispensable for the teacher in order to introduce him to a new way of seeing; otherwise, he would have no solid ground under his feet for further questions by the students. He must be able to base his conceptions, carefully considered, on an extended field of perceptions. It's different for students: They certainly want to evaluate and establish, not out of a carefully controlled process of construction, but out of insights flashing up out of the circle of their own experiences. They certainly want hints and, upon occasion, an awareness that the concepts taught them are good judgments and are well-founded. But, they don't seek systematics or proof, rather a thinking which is experiential, primal and spontaneous—not a cornerstone for proof. Of course, proof must be given and the teacher must know it, but he should not lecture incessantly afterward.

Thereby it is clear how we can abbreviate: Dispose of systematics for the teacher; dispose of half the experiments. What appears to the teacher as most graspable, most characteristic, remains as a residue. That which is omitted can be recalled in great sweeping brush strokes and summarizing thoughts. For the few students who desire a definite systematic structure, or who want material for knotty reflection and love abstract summarizing-thinking, a great deal more of the systematically based material can be woven in on the side. With experiments, one should not bring in too much nor omit too much. For each experiment, there should be time to lovingly work it up, to present it in its fullness.

Grade 6 Overview

CURRICULUM INDICATIONS

After that dry sketch of the basis for a phenomena-based approach and curriculum outline, let us now consider Rudolf Steiner's curriculum indications specific to the 6th grade. In Gabert & Niederhäuser's 1969 edition is a list of six key points:

(1) We begin physics instruction in the 6th grade in such a way that we tie in to all that the children have achieved through the music teaching.

(2) We begin the physics lessons by allowing acoustics to be born out of the musical.

(3) Also you thoroughly link acoustics to the study of musical tones and then go over to a description of the character of the human larynx.

(4) You may not yet describe the human eye here, but you may describe the larynx.

(5) Then we go over to optics and heat science—in that you take up only the most important things.

(6) Also the fundamental concepts of electricity and magnetism should be brought into the sixth grade class.[3]

HOW THE STUDY UNFOLDS THROUGH THE YEAR

According to this, physics should not at all be pursued in the usual sense—so physically; rather, it **ought to take up the musical in a suitably broad way**. In short, acoustics will not only be built on but rather **born out of the musical**. This "giving birth" is to be made an experience in the lessons; that is, we need to clearly work through each of the individual steps. To give birth means: Initially, the acoustics is one with the music, then acoustics becomes separate, without becoming detached. With this we don't mean music in general, but "what the children have achieved [made their own] through the music classes," that which has become musical capacities in the children's soul, and has also become concepts (music curriculum). Along with this, we should think about the "study of musical tones."

The second thematic and methodological footing toward which acoustics reaches should be the discussion of the larynx. Therewith, something is introduced which could be seen as a topic in an ordinary physics, namely: the genesis of tones (and certainly including how they are formed by the human being in instrument construction, in theatrical arts, and by a keyboard organ); also, to a lesser degree, topics of sound expansion, reflection and attenuation (which will be brought more fully in later grades).

Acoustics becomes physics in that it brings the audible into connection with other senses and outer data and also is not limited, like the pure study of sound, to mere hearing. **Acoustics here shall not be built up out of natural phenomena—** for example, from the resounding of wood, the rustling of water—**but from cultural phenomena.** The sounding and sighing of the world is something derived. The most primal, all-encompassing and highest in the world that we hear is the musical; it is the whole from which we should proceed. The creative, primal power of music, which comes down from antiquity, is sung, for example, in the Kalevala as the singing and playing of the kantela or lyre.

The description of the larynx, which is indicated for study next, leads further into a region which, as such, is not yet dead nature-phenomena, but rather—like music—receives function and sense through human activity and intention.

The curriculum indication ends with a mere enumeration of the topics to be handled in addition. A series is given, first leading to optics; it is questionable whether color theory is included with "optics." The conventional school optics of Steiner's day brought in the genesis of color more toward the end of the class. Perhaps this first physics block ought not concern itself at all with color optics, but rather with the customary introductory physics topics, e.g., with so-called light sources and expansion of light—only considered using a different method.

From a certain viewpoint, **music** originates from between the spirit and soul; **optics** and color experiences from between soul and body; **warmth** arises in between body and the physical; and finally, **electricity** originates beneath the physical forces. This path of incarnation, alluded to in the order of topics indicated by Dr. Steiner, can occur again in many of the sub-topics in that a person passes from the inclusive connections (music) to the objective characteristics, e.g., to the string length which determines a single tone.

However, it is characteristic that above all even the physical aspects of musical tone are not entirely material. For it is not a matter of numbers as a quantity with units of measurement, such as kilograms or meters, but a matter of number relationships, independent of absolute magnitude. The units are simplified away, usually leaving dimensionless proportions (fractions) of small, whole numbers.

Therein we link on to the Greek history block. To the people of this pre-Christian culture, the form element, beautiful well-proportioned form, not the substance, was the reality. Music expresses itself in true proportion (the interval) in the small whole numbers, which are complete in their simplicity. That must have interested the Greeks, and it is well adapted to this phase of life in the 6th grade. If, in the 6th grade, one attempts to keep the students free of a premature object-science and technical experiments derived therefrom, then in the end the students will genuinely note the lack of mechanistic explanations and technical-experimental explanations. It appears to them that this 6th grade physics is missing something: the marvelous apparatus, which brings the invisible to light out of the world, which our world then "explains." For the prevailing cultural dogma has long had the children in its grasp, instilling subconsciously the view that out of their own perceptions and a healthy human intellect, they can never attain to knowledge of the "ground of existence."

Such thoughts are unavoidable for many students today. However, one can make an adjustment with the chapter on electricity. There, everything naturally comes to view through apparati and flashy demonstrations, and such doings are well-suited. If necessary one can give the study of electricity more weight. For many students—not only the hobbyist—it is the most interesting topic of the block. If one wants the most enchanting experiments, then perhaps omit He4b, He5 and He6 and pull in, possibly, the student experiment He10 from grade 7—depending on the students' needs.

In order to make the didactics understood, speak in preparation at the parent evenings. And, one can help oneself by giving the block as a new unit near the beginning of grade 6, and not deferring it to later in the year.

Grade 6 Acoustics

I. ACOUSTICS BORN OUT OF MUSIC

1.1 HIGH AND DEEP STRING SOUNDS

If possible, juxtapose a double bass, cello, and violin; then, without any sort of explanation at a glance, we thus give the students a direct-experience perception of the differences from one to the next. Then a selection of a string quartet (perhaps played to the students by the class teacher or music tutors) could be listened to several times over—with the challenge to observe the following about the height and depth of tones:

- Which instrument sounds forth with the most rapid tone sequence, i.e., the most pronounced melodic element?
- Which instrument shows a preference to sound forth the slow beat with strength and certainty?
- Next, observe how the hand is active. It isn't the bow-movement which alters the tone, but the left hand does it in an astonishingly difficult placement or tremolo.

At the same time we note:
- On which instrument are these finger motions light and easily executed, and where do they become arm motions which initiate great waves of music and take a longer time?
- Observe the to and fro motion of the bow (with the double bass, the strokes are large sweeps, emphatic, powerful, often quiet).

We also make the observation that in contrast to the cello and double bass, the violin is based on a different body size. It would be significant for the children to receive an exact mental picture of (perhaps also to experience) how one holds each instrument. Some may already know from their experiences in instrument classes.

Then, we listen as the individual instruments are played. The double bass produces for us a music very extreme at the low-tones end and the highest violin tones produce an upper extreme. (Compare extremes in nature: the heavy step of farm horses, the twittering of the tiniest birds.) We compare not only high and deep tones, but high and low music. And, the things thus discovered we connect again to the other sense perceptions and also note the consequences of, e.g., the size of the instrument, different movements in play, positioning the instrument on the body, etc. (Also, contrast the qualities we feel lead to "more incarnated" music and "less incarnated.")

As we leave behind the melodic and come to the highest tones, they pull us out of the earthly world, they "excarnate" us. Coupled with the quick changes and running, sprightly movements of middle tones, they awaken the upper man. Through right musical use the excarnation is sustained—consciousness grows.

In the reverse, the low tones lead us into an experience of the earthly *and* mighty, they incarnate us into the will. Their right musical use strengthens our force of action, our resolution. With an improper application, it can imprison the will or stir it up (e.g., the drum background of youth mass organizing of the totalitarian state, rock music). In contrast, weak tones and slowly drawn out deep tones tend to put us to sleep. So, both ranges of tone each have their bright and dark sides, their special possibilities and their dangers.

A few more topics remain to be woven in—perhaps in the music period—as to the musician's profession, instrument technology, and also the cultural history of the violin builder, for example.[1]

1.2 EPISTEMOLOGICAL ASIDE

The physicist might object here that the indicated division into high and contrasting deep realms of tones is totally subjective and would view the frequency scale [not presented in grade 6] as going unbroken from zero to infinity. It becomes clear that we aren't dealing primarily with the physical, outer frequencies, but rather with our experience of hearing, which is based on other, wholly experiential, perceptions or sensations. Actually, the human being is oriented to a middle condition of pitch; we always experience the tones in relation to one another and to this middle position. Also, when high and low notes don't sound in simultaneous contrast, we introduce this sense of interval ourselves, since we are aware of it and live in the middle condition. It is **this inner sense,** primarily, which allows us to say: That is a high [or low] tone.

It would be an error to judge physically that a particular tone (for example, a high one) is the non-qualitative, objective reality, and the sensation that it is "high," called forth by a deep tone sounding just prior or after, as something subjectively arrived at. It is much more within the truth—that is, self-evidently, within the world of musical pitch—that tones follow one another and are connected to one another. It is relative experience, musically speaking, that is our reality. On the other hand, the individual tone, in the usual physical sense, has fallen out of this connection, so it cannot stand at the beginning nor at the end of the acoustical studies in this block.

In this, we strive for **a particular mode of apprehending reality.** To learn such a mode has decisive consequences for all the subsequent natural-scientific lessons. The entirety of music, the musical surroundings, is the higher reality; out of it fall, or fell, all the tones and sounds: the sighing of the grass, the yowling and moaning of forests on a stormy night, the murmuring of a brook, the percussive clanging of a metal plate or glass. The teaching later goes into individual examples of these sorts of natural tones and sounds, which do not lend themselves to ordered relationships and musical formation but afford a feeling for the object (especially its inner condition). But, prior to this, it is important to have plunged into a wholly musical acoustics. Thereby, given such a decision on a starting point which says, "The true beginning of sound is formed music," we can have a direction which allows us to order the phenomena in a consequent way. For, with music, one proceeds at the same time from the higher man, from his cultural activity.

1.3 HIGH AND DEEP ON OTHER INSTRUMENTS

Now, we might pursue with other instrument families how, as deep tones and large forms arise, a great force or a mighty air stream is necessary. We examine or recall instruments such as:

- flute
- trumpet or horns
- trombone
- pipe organ
- lyre
- clavichord

We can then investigate specifically how, for deep tones, the stringed instruments have much thicker strings and resonate much longer. They resonate much less, as we have already seen, in lively melodies. At the same time we experience how the deep tones must incarnate deeper in things which are large and massive: A sizable mass must be set into motion with a low piano string—and how far-reaching is the vibration! Compare the large excursion of the vibration of, for example, a tympani with the string of a violin. With the piano, the comparison is much less visible: The powerful percussion of the hammer required by a large, deep-sounding string is partly produced by the operation of the key and hammer mechanism. Concealed from the player, the hammer for the lower strings is nevertheless much more massive than for the higher ones.

Alongside the principle of "large and small produce deep and high," one also should make conscious how the specific material has a share in the sounding-character: Lead and silver differ from wood; there is no such thing as a lead violin or a wooden trumpet.

If one has developed a clear perception of these sizable differences, then one can draw attention to one of the most significant phenomena of acoustics which, although simple, is difficult to grasp. The realization of it brings the most diverse instruments to the same tone. Despite entirely different sounding characteristics, different instrument constructions, and different tone-developing and release mechanisms in all these instruments (and voices), we nevertheless can establish one tone which goes through them all. As a physical resonance, this single tone is passed from one instrument to another. (If possible don't show anything here yet of the tuning fork on resonance-boxes experiment.) **This "sympathy of the phenomena" is characteristic for the realm of sound:** Something interweaves throughout the separate individual sounds. Here we allude to the fact that if the students do not listen for this unifying aspect of musical sound, only mechanical concepts will work on them. And, unfortunately, living experience is often replaced with such "vibration" concepts (or the one-sided "frequency" concept).

With all of these considerations, we don't yet ask how the pitch is related numerically to the length of a string under tension or to a sounding air column; we see only qualitatively, woven into the play of music, how the stretched string or blown part of the flute is shortened. Along with the string thickness, we can add the tension and strength as two additional variables which will affect tone. One can draw the children's attention to how halving the free length of a string raises the tone one octave. But, for a beginning, one is then already too far outside the musical, since from the double bass to the violin the tone is raised not merely by fingering (shortening) but by a **metamorphosis to a different and delicate instrument form** (the violin). In the realm of this new gestalt, the tension and strength of the strings are altered, so that **the tone** not only becomes higher, but **also sounds entirely differently.** And therein lives music and the pitch embedded in it, as is the focus for us at first in the imagistic overview of instrument construction and playing. Only then, as a second step, the non-artistic investigations follow, which aim at the abstract physical pitch and length relationships.

One can investigate the high/deep relationships further with choral voices. One could finally express the discoveries in this way: In reaching toward higher tones, the larynx unconsciously becomes inwardly tense (which trained singers strive to avoid) and the neck is shortened. Fine, delicate and outwardly small larynxes are very capable of this (and the reverse). But such a rule is not decisive. More important is for the students to detect the quality of the high tone: the celestial brightness, the mobility and quickness in the play of melody, a bell-like clear tone, which has (in a visual analogy) a sparkling, flashing character, and that they connect this quality with an outer image of something small, tensed, delicate (choir boy vs. stocky opera star). They gain then a purely qualitative experience of tone through the perceptions of other senses. The discovery harmonizes with the considerations of larger and smaller instruments. What has been taken up by other senses becomes a musical physics.

1.4 PEDAGOGICAL THOUGHTS

The birth of acoustics out of music seems very possible, even simple to organize, but can easily turn into a fiasco. The teacher sees the enrichment from the many-sided connection with music. She dwells happily in it, since she knows her way here. The children are disappointed, since nothing "physics-like" occurs. The birth must not come to a standstill. A person must courageously forge on ahead into the subsequent material; **acoustics may last at most one week** (in a 4-week block). Also, for example in the instrument construction topic, one should strive to bring something strikingly new, and thereby the students won't experience that the material in the block is already well-known (music) merely rearranged (acoustics).

A physics class which begins immediately with startling equipment and novel effects makes things easy at first. However, we are striving here for something else: a deeper level of interest in the class. With such an imagistic montage, the teacher will seek to present things in a clear, understandable way, and foster an acquaintance with what can be observed objectively in the outer world.

II. ABOUT THE ORIGIN OF TONES

2.1 THE OCTAVE (RATIO & PROPORTION)

In the first step, we listened to music. The finely sculpted, weightless music of higher tones can be connected with the delicate, small instrument forms; correspondingly, earthy-solid music with the lower tones. Now, we leave behind the realm of the choral and symphonic; and, from its interweaving with music, **we cut up the music and extract the tone scale.**

Play the major scale from middle C downward to the ninth and tenth tone below middle C (B & A). Already with the eighth tone, the students will experience a completion of the first tone-series. Deeper tones will be experienced as the beginning of something new. Students know about this already from the music lessons. The **octave encompasses** all tones of a similar kind; **it is a whole.** Does this whole also appear outwardly, e.g., in the string length of a cello?

One fingers a C-string (without a dampener) exactly at the middle, and challenges the students to follow the length of the bowed portion, as one passes down through the tones (C, B, A, ...). At the octave, the length is double: The whole string is active. When we come thus to the open length, we hear the beginning tone again, but an octave lower; we have stepped through a unity. To demonstrate the exact midpoint of string length, one can clamp a paper strip folded in half under the string. Also the direct doubling of a string length can now be investigated on other strings and on other instruments. (Here we need not yet deal with the small error in the length-relationship which occurs due to pressing the string down onto the fingerboard, changing thereby its length and tension.)

Now, how does one achieve yet lower octaves? As you know, by the following: For example, first bow a string at 1/3 its length (damping the 2/3 portion); then double it (fingering now the 2/3 portion)—the octave sounds; now lengthen the bowed string by 1/3 (playing now the whole string)—the fifth below sounds, not another octave! In light of this we can't maintain the notion that the octave is a definite length: We can even distinguish octaves within the middle of a string length. Restated: **The harmony** (consonance) **of intervals depends** not upon an absolute string length, but rather **upon its relationships** to what surrounds it.

For the sequence of thinking, it is usually immaterial whether the experiments of this portion are played upward or downward. What has been indicated transcends the measure of the senses. However, each sequence has a different soul effect upon the students; for example, stepping downward acts in a calming, consolidating manner (best for a sanguine class, etc).

Summarized, as we have shown experimentally, every octave has its own **relative length:** half of the preceding, double the following.

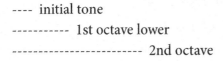

```
---- initial tone
----------- 1st octave lower
----------------------- 2nd octave
```

And, also, within each octave, the steps of whole tones on the string grow larger going downward, as can be shown by playing the scale. In a twofold way, it is so that:

- for the lower octave tones, the string is ever longer;
- between lower octave tones, the steps on the string grow ever larger, the further downward we go.

So now we understand the curving form of the horns, the harp, and others, although the quadratic equation [exponential series] governing string length as a function of different tension and string thickness comes to expression only dimly in the construction of these instruments.

The absolute string length in centimeters **corresponding to a particular tone can never be specified.** It depends on the type and tension of the string. Only the length relationship of two tones (e.g., forming a fifth) can be specified. Here, we find the musical principle again: **The significant thing lies between the tones.** Only the connection two tones have with each other is unequivocal (i.e., by length relationship).

Now, on a violin, one could step downward through the octaves, playing double strings and taking up the tone on a following string, until it goes no lower. And, there, one bumps into another musical fact: On one individual instrument, all octaves are not possible; rather, one apportions them among the large and small instruments. For, it is not only the abstract string length which determines the tone (as is suggested by the traditional and truly unnecessary school monochord) but rather, for a musical tone-condition, a particular instrument with its own individual form is necessary. Tapping on the back of a violin or cello, we can hear how the **whole body of the instrument answers**—how the tension penetrates the whole instrument body. The plates of the instrument are also under tension, and the body has a definite measure, as does the string. So, after the rationalism of the string length measurements, the mystery of genuine instrument craftsmanship surfaces once again—the mystery of music, which employs a body for incarnation; which is to say, music needs something more than just exactly measured, tensioned strings.

2.2 INTERVALS AND NUMBER RELATIONSHIPS (MUSIC & MATH)

In the 6th grade, one ought not to cover one interval after another. Rather, after the octave and the fifth, lay aside the consideration of string lengths. Already with these two, one can draw **the fundamental phenomena of the tone series: the simple whole number ratios.** The string lengths are related not by any sort of fraction (perhaps something in thousandths), but rather by the first, simplest, integral numbers (1:2, 2:3, etc.)! One can rejoice that the cosmos is so comprehensible! For a deeper understanding, one must certainly ask what these numbers signify as they relate to the human being. As E. Schuberth presented in summary [*Erziehungskunst 4/1976, p.144*], our concept of number has been developed from our sense of movement! With three repeated arm movements, the child indicates three things—thus the number arises out of the numerical rhythms of self-movement. If we consider the intervals and the movement sense, we can find how dance steps describe intervals: three steps forward, two to the side—the fifth? The interval lengths point further to rhythm, to a time sequence. The ever-new temporal-rhythmical existence of music is discovered again out of the numerical string length relations.

The simple whole number ratios of string lengths, however, point to a greater organism. Such numbers as 1:2, 3:4, etc., are close neighbors; they build on one another. Their objective connections are rhythmically imparted. For any one tone, all other tones of the string stand in close relation to it. Each individual tone also has, within its bodily length-measure, an orientation to all others, and thus to the greater whole; none falls out [of such connection]. One to two gives the octave, two to three the fifth, three to four the fourth, four to five the (major) third, three to five the sixth. Tones are not, as are material bodies, individualized, separated, tossed apart. Also, their tangible, purely physical "objectiveness" (the length) remains linked in a clear relationship. Our musical tones resemble more the brightness and order of the heavens, which ever points toward the whole; much less do they resemble the confused individuality of terrestrial forces. Such thoughts concerning string lengths, the part and the whole, support the ancient story of a harmony of the spheres.

In connection with Kepler's ideas oriented to a cosmic harmony of the planetary spheres, and if it is necessary for the students to follow the connection, one can tie onto something objective: octave calculations. If we take the fifth of the fourth, for example, then we get our first interval: the octave. Why? Arithmetically expressed:

$$2/3 \times 3/4 = (2 \times 3)/(3 \times 4) = 6/12 = 1/2$$

The fourth is therefore called an "inversion" of the fifth. What about the third of the major sixth? The calculations go as follows:

$$3/5 \times 4/5 = 12/25$$

This falls just sharp of the octave, which should be $(12.5)/(25)$. If we survey the keyboard, we recognize: The sixth is short of the octave by a minor third; from B to C is a half tone. The minor third has a string ratio 5:6. Thus the computation runs:

$$3/5 \times 5/6 = 15/30 = 1/2$$

One can also ask the reverse: What length ratio must exist for the interval between the major sixth and the octave of a primary tone?

$$3/5 \times R = 1/2 \text{ or}$$
$$R = 1/2 \div 3/5 = 1/2 \times 5/3 = 5/6$$

It is also noteworthy that the relationship of string lengths must be expressible with numbers lower than 7 if we do not want dissonance. The ratios discussed here form the natural **diatonic scale.** The "tempered" scale of our modern music is easily postponed, except that already [in the diatonic scale] a discord arises; see further in the literature. It is also interesting that the primary intervals arise in human speech: The male voice falls in puberty about an octave, the female about a third. With a question, the voice rises at the end of the sentence about a fifth; with an assertion, it falls about a fourth.

From such intervals presumably arises the expression to be "in tune" or "harmonious." Alternatively, "doesn't sound right" means there is error or deceit. The ideal of the Good and the True, toward which we strive, is dimmed and not active when we say something is "out of tune." The thing does not reveal itself, shows no clear relationship, is concealed. Analogously, so it is in music. If tones are not in "harmony," the simple, clear relationships are adulterated. The intervals are also an example of one sort of harmonizing of differing phenomena, also in the sense of the comparison that in the corporeal world (with string lengths), simple and clear relationships prevail where harmonious relationships prevail.

About small whole numbers, the renowned classical physicist Hermann von Helmholtz writes (in *Concerning the Physical Basis of Musical Harmony*, 1857):

> It has always absorbed me, as a wonderful and especially fascinating mystery, that in the science of sound, the physical and technical basis of music, which acts more basically upon the human soul than all other arts and appears as the most insubstantial, mobile and delicate creator of incalculable and indescribable sounds, [music] shows itself so fruitfully to mathematics, the science of pure and consequent thought...
>
> Mathematics and Music, with the strongest contrast of spiritual activity known to man, and yet bound up together, supporting each other, as if they wished to allude to the mysterious consequences, which permeate throughout all the activity of our spirit, also allowing us in the revelations of artistic genius to intuit an expression of a mysterious intelligence of which we are normally unaware.

Helmholtz includes a brilliant, understandable lecture on the concept of sound waves and the creation of sounds through superimposition of oscillations—as he saw it. Most interesting points are contained in it concerning instrument construction, overtones, the correspondence of voices, and such.

Fundamentally, Helmholtz regarded the small whole numbers of string length relationships in such a way that he classified both the origin and activity of sound in the human being as a kind of unconscious, subjective harmony, which must be alluded to through the spiritual activity of mathematics. Instead of a sundering of man and world or a proposed mystical unity, we seek a common point in the observation of our thinking.

2.3 OSCILLATION PHENOMENA

Key ideas: Blurriness, freeing from solidity with persistent motion.

Anyone who has received a contemporary physics education will, beneath everything covered so far, have the gnawing question: Doesn't all this depend upon oscillation, on vibrations heard by our ears? Here is one side of the false reality-concept of a material-causal worldview—as though it is not the tone, but material oscillations which are "real." (see Section 1.2. above) Again, attention is drawn to a justified phenomenological principle of musical instruments and genesis of tones, that can be understood above all (in the 6th grade) without resorting to a concept of mechanical vibration (and experiments designed for finding it) but rather out of basic experiential observations.

We have already observed that when a cello string is bowed, the shape blurs! And, certainly, it is the bowed portion, not the fingered part, which blurs. A finger touched carefully to it will be made to vibrate. Also, the violin back vibrates. Even a paper box completely closed on all sides (about a shoe box size)—freely held between the fingertips—will begin to vibrate, to hum with the sounding of choral singing.

All this does not show that such vibrations are the true source of tones and the spreading out of tones, but simply that a second phenomenon (blurring) comes into play which we have to bring into connection with the idea of intervals and harmony. In the vibrating and blurring of the shape, one has the experience that the restful, solid-bounded condition is somewhat "disembodied," i.e., becomes formless and altered in the transition. At the same time a lightweight foreign body can be flung away upon touching [the sounding body]: We encounter thus an inner movement; however, without a lasting alteration and without having been displaced finally from its initial position.

This is related to the way movement has been artistically brought into the instrument. The cello stands with a pointed foot on the ground; the knees hold only its cheeks, and its back and belly remain free. The violin is suspended in the air. One imagines that if sand were piled up over the strings and only the place where the bow stroked the string peeked out, no tone would arise, only a weak, rasping sound. The harp string, the bell of the trumpet, the bar of the xylophone, the horn of the trombone or the vault of a cymbal, all must stand free in the air. Moreover, they must also be inwardly solid, tensioned, and elastic, their form constantly resisting impacts, blowing, or bowing. Pulpy, moist, leaden things don't ring. Thus we require an objective solidity, which must, however, not be embedded in the surroundings. Best if it rests on the earth on only one point (cymbal, harmonica), perhaps on two points or at most only along the edges. In these physical principles—**freeing from heaviness for mobility** and **the persistent form**—what otherwise would be conceived as merely mechanical "vibration" becomes an image of the inner, artistic craft of instrument construction. And only to this degree is it good to study it in the 6th grade; the experiments with oscillation drawings on a sooty plate are deferred to the 7th grade.

With wind instruments, the musician works with the most mobile thing that he can utilize: his own breath. (We say "breath" for that which proceeds from us, enlivened; the word *air*, in contrast, is abstract, referring to that which occupies space.) The breath penetrates freely into the surroundings, it streams. That naturally leads not to the ending of tones (for this requires rigidity, maintaining a location), but to mobility, though not a moving-away nor a transporting. The instrument builder here conceives the reverse: He does not make it free but closes it up in order to make a node (stable point).

In considering vibrations in this manner, as the blurring of the object, we find a material image of music: Something occurs, intensively penetrates all bodies, removes their boundaries and their separateness, shapes mighty soul processes— and then disappears, leaving behind no physical changes at all!

2.4 CHLADNI FIGURES, HOMEMADE INSTRUMENTS

A practical, visualizable image of the mysterious and intricate structure of such vibrations is given by the Chladni sound figures.[2] A black lacquered circular piece of steel, about 12" x ¾", as well as a square plate, about 11" x ¾", are fixed firmly in the center. The bow must be well rubbed with bass-rosin. At first, note the shrill tone which is higher with the smaller plate. Then, sprinkle fine sugar or fine sand using a salt shaker (if possible, filtered through a fine tea sieve). An additional dusting of lycopodium (spores) powder on the plate, upon making it sing, will swim like a cloud over the oscillating regions, which simultaneously become free of the sandy material. The oscillation forms which arise depend on how lightly a finger touches the round plate, and how far away from the bow one leads the sand line (nodal line) by such touching. The rectangular plate is first damped (by touch) at the corner. The students really love it when, after the lesson, they are allowed to bow their own figures on smaller (20cm or 8" round or square) plates. Unfortunately, one cannot show the quickly changing figures which occur while the violin is being played, since the sand glides off the domed surface. [Note: Using (laser) light, Prof. Carleen Hutchins has made these resonance forms visible to study the construction secrets of master violin-makers; *Scientific American,* October 1981. – Trans.]

The Chladni standing-wave patterns speak for themselves: Their image is a "whole form" [*gesamtgestalt*]. And yet the need might arise to causally explain the figures, particle by particle, although this fosters the [conventional] vibration concept discussed above: The sand-free regions vibrate; the sand lines are quiet areas where the plate doesn't vibrate and the sand is not shaken away. Yet, in the sand image lies also the imprint of an invisible form, painted out of movement and stillness. In any case, the causal chain should be halted here, so that one doesn't ask about the cause of the cause (cause of wavelength and frequency), but rather takes the vibration form as a phenomenon brought forth by bowing, the imprint of tone into the form which accompanies the tone. Here, as in other cases, the question about the material cause (vibration image) always leads us to a better manipulation of the material, since one now understands: (1) by touching, one creates a still place (sand-collecting), and (2) by bowing, a vibrating place (sand-removing). The grasped or fixed place forsakes its magical activity; it becomes rationally understandable. That gives us power to shape the phenomena at will.

HOMEMADE STRING INSTRUMENTS are foolproof to make, but don't sound so well. Nevertheless, one can encourage the students to make one, with at least two strings, so that they can make the tones themselves. A plywood box can be constructed, with two strong end plates to hold the strings. The box is open on top, and the bridge for the strings stands on the bottom (sound-board). The viewable half will not resonate with a top. For tension, we use large wood screws: One holds the wire by a loop. We saw a slit about 1/3 way through the other screw, into which the wire is hammered using a knife. (Alternatively the wire is fixed using Uhu glue.) Other than musician's string, steel wire of 0.3–0.5mm thickness can be used, or perhaps thicker nylon cord. The wire should lie under the head of the other screw and run over a wooden bridge, placed underneath it.

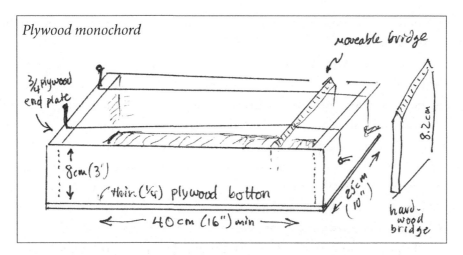

Plywood monochord

There should be an even-numbered distance between the bridges, e.g., 40cm or 16", which is easily divided into integral lengths for work with the intervals. For this we make two movable bridges, which are 1–2mm higher than the fixed ones and can be moved back and forth on the box bottom (sounding board). Often they afford a louder or fuller sound, since the bottom is now more closely tied to the vibration of the string. An extremely simple instrument consists of one tensioned wire on a board; the interval relationships can be shown even with such simple equipment.

III. THE LARYNX

3.1 EXPERIENTIAL ACCOUNT

The above-cited indication by Dr. Steiner for a description of the physical-physiological constitution of **the larynx** does not mean some sort of anatomical sketch, but a description, **an experiential account.** It also does not imply a dissection nor the anatomical contents arising therefrom, nor a study of diseases and surgical therapies of the larynx. Rather, initially, a study of experiences relating to voicebox-localized bodily activities, which then aid a physical understanding. Thereby, the larynx will be seen in the light of living processes, in light of the physiological, not as a naked, physical-anatomical kind of apparatus. For example, after an introduction by the teacher, the children can be led to observe the following:

1. The consonants are formed in the mouth with the help of a very minimal musculature, lips, teeth, tongue and gums. The consonants can be arranged in such a way that one moves from outside inward. Most, however, occur in the more frontal (outer) speech apparatus; thus the deaf can read speech from outside. Limb

and metabolic organs are here built into a speech apparatus. Use of these limbs must be slowly learned by every young child.

2. If you begin with the vocal series U, O, I (ih), E (eh), A (ah), you move backward in the throat, into the nasopharyngeal cavity. Also, you manifest those forms which simultaneously occur down the upper part of the larynx. The A(ah) forms the threshold into pure tones, into singing (la-la, tra-la, not lo-lo). In A(ah), speech sounds like singing. If the children say A(ah) themselves—perhaps in choir—they can sense how this sound is created in the depths of the larynx, and how the activity, the locality taken hold of by the body is displaced still deeper if instead of speaking the A(ah) one sings it.

3. Singing demonstrates in practice how we work from the larynx, that is, from the deepest region. With all this, nothing happens without an air stream. It shows itself as a stream penetrating outward, which at the same time always carries forth the inner contents of the soul. Thus, people are frequently embarrassed to sing.

You can lead the children through part of the following investigations about the larynx; but, better if they are assigned to try them out at home:

- Try to find the range of the human voice (approx. 3 octaves).
- Search out the pitch where singing is as loud as possible, yet still pleasing (middle range).
- Attempt to sing tonelessly, i.e., in a whisper. (The tone range you can produce is much reduced; the tones hiss and are artistically unusable.)
- See what changes when you speak in a whisper. (All possibilities of understanding speech are retained, the loudness still is malleable, and it's clear that only the voiced sounds—hard consonants—are unharmonious.)
- See if you can sing with a closed mouth and nose. (it happens only when one gradually fills the cheeks with air and also an air stream is moved through the throat. And, certainly, one needs an exhaling stream; an inhaling one forms only garbled sound.)
- Lay an ear on: the chest, lower neck, and throat; investigate where the tone arises while singing with the same volume.

Now we approach the genesis of tones in the throat by comparison to a wind instrument, e.g., a recorder. However, this doesn't exactly correspond to what we experience: We don't achieve higher tones by shortening an air column, as with a flute (nor, by singing with our mouth set to a very small round opening, or regulating the pitch of our trilling by bulging our cheeks or changing the volume of our mouth). Ordinarily we achieve high tones through creating a tension deep down in the larynx. One can imagine something thin, ribbon-like, which in singing or in speaking is more or less tense.

There is only one instrument family, the brass family (horns, trumpets, trombone, and the like), where the tensioned part—the lips of the player—is intentionally controlled during playing. The tension on stringed instruments and on drums is adjusted (tuned) only before playing. But the trumpeter is a part of the instrument with his cheek muscles. He can, thereby, ray out his will especially strongly—he is able to incite to the hunt or to battle (one thinks of the trumpeters of the apocalypse). These brass instruments, when they are massed together, pass beyond the bounds of music. With a fire-brigade marching band, the dogs howl as the brass instruments resound. The human organ of voice is far superior to such extremes in its capacity for transformation—it encompasses the range from the shrill, bellowing voice of the commander to the delicate lover's whisper.

If you wish to go further into the formation of the voicebox, you don't need dissected anatomical examples to do it; its function can be illustrated by the double reed of the oboe—with the restriction that no similar tension arises there. The human nasal tone is also most closely akin to the timbre of the oboe. With this as background, we can perhaps characterize the human larynx as the most living, unified and archetypal image of the various instrument groups—especially the wind and string instruments, for their tones can be artistically guided by a human being in the fading-away or diminuendo. In contrast, the percussion and plucked instruments permit only a dampening at the end of their tones, a stopping-short by touch-contact, not completely formed in their diminuendo or softening. Here, the softening depends more on mechanical laws.

The idea of the human voice as a synthesis of the various sounds of the orchestra can lead to the idea of arranging the instrument families of the classical orchestra in the image of the membering of the human being into head, limb, and chest regions. If, together with the students, one listens to the specific, distinctive tone colors of the various instruments, then one may feel one's way a little into this membering. Should we let all this be compresssed into a [mere] drawing of a dissected larynx? However, if at the same time one first recalls the historical situation, the atmosphere and danger of the first dissections of a corpse (recall Rembrandt's *Anatomy Lesson of Doctor Tulp*), then one may be permitted, no doubt, to do an anatomical drawing of the larynx. In any case, the throat and mouth parts which the students can see from outside could be drawn in profile. On the basis of the considerations we have described, and the investigations with one's own body, the well-known roundish swelling below the throat is aptly termed the larynx [in German, *Kehlkopf*, literally, the "head-of-the-throat"].

3.2 PHENOMENOLOGY & ROMANTICISM: A SUMMARY

We could ask, in conclusion: How do the other beings and processes of nature create sound? If one thinks of the voices of animals and the rushing of water or air and of the sounds we create with various things by striking or rubbing, we notice innumerable characteristics, but especially that the inner condition, the "soul" of the thing is revealed—however, never with the variability with which the tones of human song and speech reveal the inner condition of that source. All other sounds of the world (bodily or instrumental) are based on human sounds, not the other way around! The great unity of the musical, the harmony of the spheres, is split up in the rushing and sounding of the inanimate world:

harmony of the spheres	←mythos
voice, song, instrument individual speech, "color" of instrumental tones	←culture
animal sounds rushing, sighing	←nature

IV. UNIFIED OVERVIEW

The path described in the curriculum for the 6th grade leads analytically from the whole (music) into the parts, i.e., to the physical investigation of individual sounds. The didactic construction is:

Formed world of sound, music

High and deep realms of sound in their character with one another, seen in the image of various instrument sizes, various mobilities of the instrument bodies, etc.

Paired high and low tones in their interval and accordance relationships in the image of length relationships, length intervals

Individual tones at the border of music in the image of the Chladni vibration figures; sound as creator of form. (The reverse would be: mechanical oscillation as the cause of sound and former of tone.)

Individual tones on the way to music in the activity of the larynx

Individual sounds outside of music, which allow one to feel into the inside of the thing (broken cup, different woods, etc.)

If one doesn't begin with music as a higher unity, but with the single sounds, then one tears the child too soon out of the whole, cuts off his path to it for the time being, and moreover cannot work through the necessary analytic process. This is materialism. For, without saying it, one presupposes: The whole is the sum of the parts (and only the physical parts). Then, it makes no decisive difference whether one starts out with the sounds of natural things and various materials, or from the pure, sterile fundamental sound of a monochord and its frequency, overtones, and the like.

In the first case, the individual character of percussive sounds still lets the elemental sense perceptions be comprehensively grasped, though mixed with romanticism. (see Eichendorff's poem, "There sleeps a song in every thing...," p.47) If, however, one proceeds decisively out of music, then in the end the percussive tones also allow a trace of music to still be considered, that is, the diminished but still distinctive characteristics [of music] which we saw, which can lead back perhaps to the Eichendorff poem as a conclusion to acoustics. Ralph Waldo Emerson's "Music" is another good example.

V. LITERATURE ON ACOUSTICS

[Selected works, all still in German; perhaps if someone can translate them locally, they may be of use. – Trans.]

An inclusive overview of the acoustical world of all cultures, including the work of Steiner in detail, is the life work of the famous musical scientist Hermann Pfrogner, *Living World of Tone,* Langen-Muller Pub., Munich 1976. (see p. 240, "The Character of the Intervals")

Closely related and quite usable in many portions for our style of teaching, with a clear, factually-rich presentation is: H. von Baravalle, *Physics as Pure Phenomenology,* Vol. 3, Acoustics and Optics, Troxler Verlag, Bern, Switzerland, 1951.

Along the same lines as the foundational thoughts developed here, somewhat in fruitful accordance, partly oriented in other directions, yet enriching in many sections, and quite interesting for its selection of topics, is: E.A. Karl Stockmeyer, *Concerning the Methodology of Physics Teaching,* Verlag Freies Geistesleben Stuttgart, 1961.

Experiments in Acoustics

The acoustics experiments, taking 3–4 days, are distributed throughout the preceding text. [A synopsis is given below. – Trans.]

SYMPHONIC - CHORAL

Ac1: Observing a selection played by a string quartet: Observe the qualities of each passage, how it was played, how it felt. Observe the qualities of each instrument: differences in musical sound (high: less incarnated; low: more physical strength).

Ac2: High and low notes on other instruments: flute, trumpet, trombone, saxophone, pipe organ, clavichord, piano. Observe the character of the tones of each instrument, how the music is produced, how the fingering is done. (Each instrument "sings" out of its own individual being.)

Ac3: The sounding together of an orchestra (**consonance** as a fundamental phenomenon of acoustics, unity within diversity)

INDIVIDUAL TONES – MUSICAL

Ac4: Paired tones: Consider the notes of a **major scale** downward to the 9th and 10th notes; note how the cycle feels like it completes at the 8th note. Now, observe the scale on a stringed instrument (guitar or more abstractly, monochord); note the size of successive steps on the fingerboard. (The conscious, perceiving human being as unifier in the "middle.")

Ac5: Deeper scales; intervals and harmony: Pluck a stringed instrument at 1/3 the length, then double it (2/3). Now, pluck the open string (3/3); a third note sounds—the fifth. (It is the relative length that matters. Compare the strident quality of the fifth, the harmonious quality of the third. Note how the finger steps are wider, for lower octaves; graphs as an exponential series, an ever steeper curve.)

Ac6: Other intervals and their number relations (beyond octave 1:2, fifth 2:3, perhaps also the major third, 4:5)

OTHER ORGANS OF SOUND

Ac7: Sound as forming force; **Chladni figures** as revealing the invisible, dynamic forms which are constantly created in any musical instrument (the life of music: becoming indistinct, fuzzy when sounding: formed activity)

Ac8: Investigations with the voice: singing, speaking, extreme limits, conditions of harmonious singing and speaking

Ac9: Sound in nature (descent of the harmony of the spheres): singing of the wind, bubbling brook, how high and low still sing to us. Sound reveals the inner soul condition of animals through their mewing and bellowing; it also reveals the inside of objects (characteristic sounds of brass, wooden xylophone, a broken porcelain cup).

Ac10: Poetic or speech work: e.g., Eichendorff poem, Emerson's poem, Shakespeare's sonnet on Orpheus, etc.

Divining Rod (1835)
A song sleeps in all things
Which dream on and on,
And the world begins to sing
If only you find the magic word.
  – Joseph von Eichendorff

Music
Let me go where'er I will
I hear a sky-born music still;
It sounds from all things old,
It sounds from all things young,
From all that's fair, from all that's foul,
Peals out a cheerful song.

It is not only in the rose,
It is not only in the bird,
Not only where the rainbow glows,
Nor in the song of woman heard,
But in the darkest, meanest things
There alway, alway something sings.

'Tis not in the high stars alone,
Nor in the cup of budding flowers,
Nor in the redbreast's mellow tones,
Nor in the bow that smiles in showers,
But in the mud and scum of things
There alway, alway something sings.
  – R.W. Emerson

Grade 6 Optics

HOW SHOULD WE SEEK KNOWLEDGE?

In optics, as much as in the teaching of each subject, and actually with every cultural activity, the highest goal is: *to learn to love the world more.* Contemporary school physics causes the opposite early on. Although the view of what light is has undergone many transformations since the 17th century (since Newton and Huygens), it is nevertheless a fundamental concept which has subsequently become general belief. To the modern consciousness, light is taken to mean *something* which continuously streams out from a light source in rectilinear rays and after much refraction or focusing somehow impinges upon [objects] or is reflected; i.e., light as a kind of finely-material movement. (The fundamental question: What do we think "light" is? will be explored further in 11th grade.)

Although early in its historical development physics had the goal of establishing some sort of mechanical principle as a basis for light, it now must begin to oppose such naïve ideas; for quantum physics now understands that:

- Light is not a "something" in any sort of unequivocally definable sense. It is even senseless, in a material, tangible context, to research what it actually "is."
- There can be no talk of "rays." On the one hand, light is expressed in wave phenomena, on the other hand, in "quanta."
- A continuous radiation of light has not been established; weak light sources send out energy in statistical packets or quanta.

Such contradictions[1] hardly disturb the naïve mechanical evaluation of light, nor unsettle it at all. What may not correspond (in modern quantum physics), happily persists as the layman's conviction. For, such a limited evaluation is in sympathy with a certain fundamental (though unspoken) postulate of physics: If the perception and thought of a human being were not present, all light and the brightness and darkness produced by it would still exist the same. In other words, the illuminated world is something completely finished, an external reality, sufficient unto itself. This view sees the world as outside, complete, only objectively conceived, into which the human being enters as an outsider. Inside, he fashions as objective an image of the world as he can, to the extent that he learns to conceptualize (mentally picture) the causative material processes acting among objects—believing that what he perceives and experiences of the world is only subjective [i.e., not necessarily its "real essence"]. In any event, he values such conceptualizations only as indicators, hinting at the causative processes believed to be hidden in matter. When we said earlier, "the human being may, through knowledge, learn to love the world more," we need to be more precise: to learn to love, to shape our own perceptions—not the objectivity which we imagine as *beyond* the perceptions.

Why do we study optics? In order to make the visual world richer through thought: the everyday world, not the world of a theorist, but our own. Also, in school we ought to resist seeing intricate optical instruments, cameras, motion pictures, microscopes and telescopes, which create new, amazing images for us. But first enter the images of the world by the gate of our own senses, from the starting point of our own vision. On this basis we will establish what is experienced in seeing (purely expressed—where it is bright and where it is dark, and how these relate to one another) without simultaneously saying: Light is passing by, being absorbed, reflected, etc.

Whoever does not wish to take their focus from the "manifest phenomena" of daybreak and dusk, from the whole of atmospheric optics, should in no way concern themselves with optics; but then neither should they ardently try to proffer mechanical theories (based on experimentally achieved ray processes) as fundamental concepts of the light of the world.

If a person wants to include the human being in the world and penetrate his visual connection with the world, then it is truly permissible—even necessary—to introduce entirely new visual concepts. In order to express the perceptible in a hypothesis-free way, such concepts as "light source" or "illumination direction" and the like, are not sufficient alone because they already contain all sorts of material connotations. Since the phenomena are indeterminate, *initially our concepts should remain open-ended.* Also, we should completely put out of our minds questions about the essence of light. Nevertheless, at the outset, it is worthwhile to clarify to what degree it is permissible to speak of light as a part of the whole of reality.

Certainly, unfamiliar ideas and descriptions will occur in this study of optics. However, one should evaluate each of them oneself as to whether they lead to our goal and express in a hypothesis-free way that which has been discovered and perceived in the surroundings. What has been said in a somewhat epistemological-theoretical way will receive further clarification through the following description of the actual phenomena. In order to be completely concrete, a description of the syllabus comes next (I. Beginning Lessons). In the following section (II. Seeing and the Sun) many of the underlying ideas are presented. These ideas are also discussed further by Georg Maier in the newsletter *Elemente der Naturwissenschaft*, especially volumes 2/1973, 2/1975, 1/1977; also Essay 2 in Jochen Bockemühl, ed., *Toward a Phenomenology of the Etheric World.*[2]

I. BEGINNING LESSONS

1.1 MORNING: LIGHT AS INTERWEAVING WHOLE

"And there was light." Thus the words rang forth in the fullness of Creation's morning. And *what force came into the world with light!* How does the human being live now in light and how in darkness? Before we separate out details or analyze brightness and shadow in our study of light, it is worth meeting the world of light as a whole, as a healer—seeking the experience of light. Thus, the sunrise provides one of the most profound encounters with the power of nature. Modern man accepts this daily gift of the cosmos to the earth with a sullen mood, or a demanding one, since it seems to him nothing more than a particular world-occurrence, merely a mechanical consequence of the movement of dead masses in the darkness of outer space. But something else is in fact experienced by a person when passing from darkness into the daylight.

Perhaps before the block begins, the sunrise can be experienced on a class trip;[3] alternatively, parents could collect the children at night and drive them to a sunrise. If not, one can impressively create most of the phenomena as an experiment within the classroom.

Make a basement room 100% dark (amazingly difficult). Then let the students experience as much as possible in the darkness: noise, shape, touch of roughness and coolness. Then, slowly turn on a low-power bulb: A first, pallid glimmer appears on the ceiling—the beholder's gaze may drift longingly out there, without actually being able to discern any sort of visible objects (something is invisibly happening, getting warmed up; Saturn).

Sunrise experiment, Op1

Brightened further, it seems like the distance out there gets nearer. So also with sunrise: A heaven dawns which at first seems distant; darkness still holds fast to the earth. Initially, we generally perceive planar, shadow-like forms with no depth; later we can make out indefinite, schematic, but still weakly embodied objects. However, in between the latter lies an impenetrable darkness which still envelops our gaze with sleep ("out there" is a center: sun, gray, uncolored outlines: Moon stage).

Now, the color of things first becomes visible, not yet related in brightness to the distance, but rather floating over the surface of (nearby) objects, which are still swimming in darkness. These colors do not correspond with the colors of the sky, which are still pale and dim.

Only much later are we able to clearly discern anything in the spaces in between. Now objects can be grasped, set down, or also thrown at a target with some certainty. Now (experiments below) the first shadows occur in nature. "Daylight" now prevails, and we go about our daily work (clear landscape: Earth stage).

This experience of dawn comes to expression only dimly in experiments. However, one can connect to the midday experience with the demonstration: Significantly increase the brightness by slowly increasing the power to a 1000-watt halogen lamp (set up shadowed from the students): A glistening panorama arises with various colored objects, placed there earlier on the front wall. (This concludes demonstration experiment Op1.)

In doing such experiments and the students' making such observations, a teacher must ask: How does human consciousness live in the various *stages of twilight*? How is the orientation to the world changed in the active person? In this we always mean a person with her senses turned outward into the world, not those half-sleeping, or driven. We don't want to study the subconscious, but rather to study the act and experience of perception. While we are in complete darkness, only what is nearby is tangible; smells, imaginations, feelings press in on us. Then, we greet the widths opened to us by the first glimmer and the direction it reveals in the otherwise directionless gloom—we breathe out. And when we stand in the midst of illuminated surroundings, then the darkness which pressed in right to our skin finally yields. We are again free, for we have what is necessary about us. The incredibly differentiated multitude of things in our visible world allows us to be entirely outside—and still we are entirely in here, entirely incarnated. For now there is something for our limitless mind to do: Surroundings must be identified, spatial directions themselves recognized.

The brightness that dawns at first in the glimmer of an undifferentiated tableau is split up into the multiplicity of the surroundings, on whose surfaces our mind now ignites in activity. The soul is filled with everything and at the same time distanced from everything: I feel myself in the midst of the world, free, and yet connected. This freedom lends itself to action: Something can be accomplished with the now brightly illumined objects. They can be worked with. Thus, through his work, the human being creates ever anew an intention-filled connection with this world of individual objects, which have now lost their separation.

LIGHT AS INTERWEAVING WHOLE (IN DAYLIGHT)

However, aside from entirely *outer* conscious connections (space) and wholly *inner* activity connections (our work), do the things still have their own "light connections"? Are they entirely unrelated in brightness, darkness and color, or do these elements still weakly join them together? Aside from the objective ordering by our mind, which emphasizes that-which-has-become (past), and aside from our deeds, which are future-oriented, is there also *an activity of the present, an immediate weaving, ordering of brightness, which we can call light*? Is our thinking able to realize connections in visible brightness here in the present, without presupposing bodies (i.e., without a having-become) on the one hand, or aside from fostering the [future potential of] deeds on the other? This issue of the present is the question of dawn for the natural scientist.

Already, an initial pondering of the *shadow relationships of the sun* helps us forward: All objects present in our environment are unified, directed toward the surrounding heavens and are oriented toward the sun as much with their dark and bright sides as with their shadows. We find also a unified brightness relationship in the metamorphosis of phenomena into the distance: Everything far away becomes uniformly non-spatial, flatly arranged, colors become undifferentiated (color perspective), the haziness [turbidity] increases by degrees toward the horizon (atmospheric perspective), and over it all moves the changing celestial dome, yet always connected in its passage. These phenomena surround us in all the intimate weaving of morning. It is absent in the glistening light of midday, which lets the surroundings appear hard, unconnected, stony. This noonday light is no longer weaving and fluid, but hardened and rigidified: It strikes us.

With all this consideration of how the image of the world gradually emerges into objectivity, we must take our thinking by the reins. Seeing the colors and contrasts which swim in distances, or the characteristically indeterminate, non-objective images of earthly masses seen in the first, dim delicate expression of morning's light, we are not allowed to call these experiences only subjective. But, neither should we be allowed to reject these qualities in order to visualize again some sort of day-objectivity (still unfortunately unclear) "beyond the appearances." For that would be to say: The real phenomena [have to] pierce through, governed by "dirt effects," or "haze effects," or creating illusions. For us, reality is that which works in a perceptible, sense-filled way, not as a chain of actions there outside, but rather works in me, within the tapestry of my experience of thinking. Reality is always an idea of a whole, not the material particulars; reality is a "woven" fabric, as every rock is woven out of every piece.

Thus, as a tangible movement out of the darkness of night, the sunrise draws us with the whole might of creation onto the path of the light. The mighty triumph of sunrise follows the glimmer of dawn's soft beauty. Colors spread out about us and now we sojourn in the bright land of day. Paths of light become for us paths of living. The certainty of life is founded on such experiences of the open, manifest world.

After sunrise we live with certainty in the illumined morning actively, completely human, since the delicately weaving light relates each particular thing in the world to the whole. This provides stimulus and example for our thinking and for our striving. Then as human beings we should find our way to the whole. Soon, midday drives us back with its ultra-brightness and hardness, with its making-discrete. With a class trip or such experiences duplicated in demonstration experiments, the students do not simply experience light as just another thing in the world, a useful, profitable occurrence (which is turned on at will), but they experience it as a lofty cosmic process, which first of all is united with all consciousness, all growth, etc. We let the children enter from such a gestalt into the study of light. With this, it is completely necessary to work through and discuss in front of them many individual observations, and one has every hope that in the course of the year they will repeatedly discover it anew.

If we now begin to do research into the interweaving of light and darkness, which unawares constitutes our day-consciousness (as a basis for it, as we saw), then first of all we must investigate the extent to which this day-consciousness creates an independent lightness or darkness, detached from the surroundings.

1.2 AFTER-IMAGES AND CONTRAST PHENOMENA

THE PERCEPTIVE ACTIVITY of civilized people is too much outwardly controlled and unfree. So that the students can later find the way to a saturated experience of the world, made inwardly rich for themselves, already at this age—while still so open to the senses—it is important with after-images to exercise an open, willed, concentrated, yet extended perception which carefully notes everything. With after-images, such a visual-listening is developed, e.g., if we don't tie our gaze down—as usual—to fixating on the object's edge as if to bore into it with the eyes but, instead, become awake right into the far corners, peering far and wide into the surroundings, opening ourselves to the entire panorama and experiencing how all surfaces in the field of view stand in relation to each other.

SIMULTANEOUS CONTRAST is shown first of all by presenting how a gray paper strip possesses a different gray value in a bright white surrounding than in a dark field. There is not one speck of surface in the world that can possess a constant brightness value. Everything depends upon the surroundings and thereby on the entire situation: the background, the direction of view, etc. The bark of a thin branch in front of the white-bright sky appears black; but the bark of the trunk before the sky (and also the thin branch in front of dark spruces) is gray-green, or gray, in any case not black. In nature, everything changes with the seasons, time of day, and weather. Which exact color the branches "really" have cannot be said; one must first construct a "normalized" backdrop. A certain tendency of color is definitely there: Everything doesn't swim in confusion, but in its variability with the environment, locale and time, it forms an image of the world which is lawful, although constantly fluctuating. Otherwise, everything would be isolated and rigidified; a world of finished objects, closed up in themselves, cannot stand in relation to themselves, nor to the human being, nor to the cosmos.

The constant play of delicate transformations of seen things, however, reveals such relationships. For everything strives for totality: Bright surfaces become darker against brightness, but become brighter against darkness. Everything metamorphoses toward a harmony: an equalization between brightness and darkness. [Only if we view sensations as traceable to nerve endings (which themselves, as something perceptible, are a product of sense experiences!), and choose not to see sensations as originating in the world will we be tempted to place the inhibitory cross-synapses of the afferent nerves as a fundamental, "subjective" cause of "simultaneous contrast" (after-image) phenomena.][4] This also works with color boundaries: A gray strip on a colored surface shows a subdued complementary color. All sorts of further experiments can be introduced here. (Colored shadows may be set aside in the sixth grade, because they are too difficult to clarify if we don't want to work with the yet unclear "colored light rays.")

THE AFTER-IMAGE (SUCCESSIVE CONTRAST) shows the same reaction as the surrounding contrast (simultaneous contrast): Bright becomes dark, and the reverse. Also, complementary colors reappear. Thus, after-images possess a magical, luminous light arising from very pale initial colors, a light that depends only upon our vision, and not upon external brightness. Here, we meet a color-filled, illuminating power of vision. This topic is often very popular with the students. One investigates beforehand this increasing series of phenomena. An approach to this complementarity—never fully achieved—is perhaps seen also in the dawn and sunset sky colors. The penetrating peach-orange of the sun swims over a receding turquoise ... The students can verify the colors created by the eye and by the heavens through painting a color circle.

1.3 CO-BRIGHTNESS [JOINT-BRIGHTNESS]

CONVENTIONAL CONCEPTS necessitate a prefatory remark: At least in the 6th and 7th grades, avoid speaking in terms of a radiation or movement of light, the speed of light, and above all of rays. At no time should we ascribe concepts to physical causes in order to deduce perceptions out of them, to explain them. The relationships of the visible world—as we have already seen in these few observations—show themselves to be richly differentiated, very extensive, forming a great whole. The spread-out organism of the sun-illumined world, filled to the farthest reaches with meaningful richness, should not be interpreted in terms of "light rays" which will then be thought of as focusing together. This idea conceptualized as infinitely focused, wholly and fundamentally invisible, cuts right through the infinitely spread-out world that we experience, the tapestry of the senses, which in the end is supposed to re-originate through pure addition of such foreign, atomistic rays. Herein is, after all, the attempt to constantly overlay innumerable individual [light]-paths into the manifest light which is always coherent.

These individual rays (the light rays) have nothing to do with each other, they are thought of as self-sufficient entities—although to be sure they never occur isolated as individual light or dark flecks. Certainly, we can initially develop the notion of linearity (straightness of view) based on the relationship which the edges of various lighted areas have with the light, e.g., relationships in the space behind a shadow-casting body. Nevertheless, one may not transpose these idealized elements, fashioned out of thought connections, into something physical, nor make them into a self-existing part of the world in order to designate a non-perceptible, fine materiality (rays of streaming light) as the cause of brightness.[5]

THE TANGIBLE provides a much easier opportunity for grasping the world objectively. In contrast to the *visual experience* of light, this tangibility oversteps its own realm. Light is first of all an idea of coherence, not a self-sufficient object in the bodily world—so teaches the Wave-Particle Duality of the New Physics! Since, however, light will often be popularly comprehended—also by students— exclusively as "rays," initially we ought to scarcely use the word *light*. Thereby we can educate the children to their own perceptions and independent thinking, instead of tracing back to tangible models of invisible things and purified movement (phoronomical mechanical movement). We have only indicated here how the orientation striven for clearly has a deep phenomenological basis; this has been elaborated by other researchers.[6]

THE SIMPLEST CONNECTIONS can be put into place at the onset of our light studies, aiming at uncovering the ever-present tapestry of light and darkness which surrounds us [see Op 2]. We place a sheet of paper on the table in front of us, slide it toward our clothing and bend over it: A glimmer of the color which we have on our upper body now exists on the paper. If we now hold a whiter piece of paper in front of our dark shirt (for example), the first sheet becomes whiter, brighter. We can express the phenomena thus: The more brightness there is above a surface, the brighter it is. Therewith, we have formulated brightness as a connection with its outer conditions, not caused by an inner law. We will now investigate more of such conditions.

1.4 BRIGHTNESS AND THE WHOLE ENVIRONMENT

On what does the brightness of a book cover lying on a music stand depend? If we extend the plane of the music stand (as far as is visible), we obtain a horizon plane as follows:

Everything that is bright or dark above this horizon plane stands in relationship to the surface brightness of the book cover. Brightness or darkness above the plane clearly has an effect, i.e., has a relationship to the book cover, provided we can see the bright or dark regions from the position of the book. We imagine our eye at the surface of the book cover (as if there is a tiny opening and we peer out): This view, looking out into the space surrounding

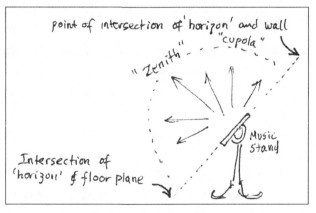

The horizon-plane around a music stand

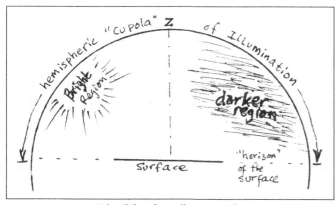

The "sky dome" or cupola

the surface, we call a "sky cupola" (half-dome). This cupola is not something made of masonry, but a dome of visibility, more precisely: a half-dome of what can be seen in the cupola. One of these "cupolas" always belongs to each surface. If there is a lamp in the room, then all those places are bright (co-bright) which have the lamp as a bright spot in their cupola; and certainly, they are brighter the larger the lamp spot appears—as seen from their place—and the nearer the lamp spot is to the cupola's zenith. We can demonstrate "horizon and cupola" for horizontal or inclined surfaces with a light bulb on a long cord (Op 2b). Step by step, we traverse the entire half-dome of the cupola—at a constant distance from the paper (see figure)—and then, finally, let the lamp pass below the horizon plane.

We can then go on to the intriguing experiment with the "all-seeing globe" (Op 3). A head-sized matte-white globe is brought into the classroom. It "accompanies" in brightness the entirety of the space before it, e.g., getting bright on the window side. Each spot on it is bright to the extent that bright objects find themselves in the half-sphere (the sky cupola) over the spot in question on the globe. That is, each spot on the globe is bright to the extent that one can see brightness looking out (from its plane) into its half-sphere (sky cupola).

And adjacent spots on the globe are, for the most part, oriented to different—although similar—sky cupolas, and therefore the globe shows gradual transitions from one spot to another. It "sees" the apportionment of light and darkness about it, and forms an image of it. We could also let a chicken egg similarly "see" its surroundings. Now, with a dark cloth, we erect a tent open toward the students, place the globe into it, and show the class that on the side corresponding to the dark interior, it gets darker (Op 4).

We designate such a brightness which follows the changes of the sky cupola as corresponding bright/dark, corresponding coloration, in short: co-bright. Into this series, however, each surface brings a constant, enduring admixture: its own color. But we don't investigate that here, since we inquire firstly into the connections to variations in the surroundings: the cupola. Every co-bright surface provides perhaps a means of distinguishing point-wise brightness in its cupola.

1.5 SELF-BRIGHTNESS / SELF-DARKNESS

Now, take this globe and invert it over the bulb (Op 5), which we power up a bit using our variable power pack; the globe gives out a ghostly glow. The connection to the surroundings is severed; even in the darkness of the tent it remains bright! Earlier, the situation was that brightness begot brightness (a brighter appearance was bestowed upon something that had brightness in its cupola); now, in spite of a dark cupola, brightness persists. Moreover, seen in front of a dark surrounding, it seems even brighter! Surfaces turned toward it are even torn out of their previous brightness connections.

This new brightness involves not only the lamp itself, but also exists in a circle about it, at the same time as at the lamp. Round about this place there exists a particular brightness hierarchy, which no longer relates to day-brightness but is oriented to the central brightness: the lamp. This brightness of the lamp which opposes the surroundings we call **"self-bright"** or self-luminous, in contrast to co-bright which follows the brightness of the cupola. To the extent that not only the lamp itself has fallen out of the connection to daylight brightness, but stands in the middle of a whole hierarchy of brightened surfaces which accompany every movement of the globe, we can also designate the globe as "self-luminous." Thereby, the phrase *light source* (which suggests a material source) is replaced by something we can meet phenomenologically, something which expresses the relationship of oriented surfaces to their surroundings, i.e., toward changes in their cupolas.

A self-bright surface can be recognized in that it is too bright for its surroundings; in terms of color differences, that is never the case with co-bright surfaces. A surface can also be shown to be self-bright in the following way: If we place a very bright spot (e.g., a lamp) in its "sky," nearer and then further away, the surface in question will not appear different. Or, one completely closes up a surface and the body carrying it inside a box: It must remain bright although cut off from heaven's brightness. Co-bright is cupola-accompanying, self-bright is cupola-opposing.

As a further investigation, we show self-darkness (Op 6): For sight (not for touch) a small aperture in a large cardboard box is a part of the visible surface of the box. This "aperture surface" remains constantly dark, despite the location or proximity of bright objects in its surrounding. Just as self-bright opposes a dark sky, so this self-dark "surface" opposes a bright sky. Only cavities with relatively small openings are self-dark; black-painted exterior surfaces, in contrast, are always somewhat bright and accompany their sky.

1.6 SKY AND EARTH

Our introduction of the visible brightness of surfaces doesn't say anything about the inner origin of brightness. It is characteristic for light that it first appears in an outer weaving. It is precisely such concepts as self-bright, co-bright, etc., which encompass that aspect of light. They are descriptions of the relationships between brightness and its cupola, as require us to principally focus on the cupola to investigate these relationships. Then we understand that what is visible from the surface is altered, i.e., the possible views from the surface, not the body itself. If, for example, we place a self-bright surface in the cupola (Op 2), that is the optical fact; the fact in tangible space is the objective lamp placed nearby. The co-bright surfaces still do have individual characteristics, specifically, their color and gray-value, i.e., gray-value as a particular capacity for co-brightness, associated with each specific body. Black bodies approach the self-dark, while white is most delicately co-bright and co-dark.

Since we wish to pursue *an optics of seeing,* not a comprehension of its *geometry,* initially we don't describe the visible things in the sky from [the viewpoint of] celestial bodies, but describe them geocentrically, even observer-centrically (relative to the viewer). These celestial bodies are non-approachable and are, not accidentally, beyond the area where such experiments apply as further shape our earthly world of phenomena. Also, it is senseless to ask, at least at first, how they would be different if they were a body which could be transposed onto black paper. Nothing at all can be asked about their connection with a possible cupola, since they themselves are our earthly cupola! Let us also work on an image of the human being on earth, accepting that we do not live there by chance. For we aren't interested in the science of some hypothetical being rocketing away from our world into the vacuum of dark extraterrestrial space. For us, *the sky is not just another self-bright object, but the all-encompassing heavenly-bright: the spread-out sun.* The sky's brightness is constantly in rhythmic pulsation. The moon shows a transition between star-type, sun-type and the terrestrial-type co-brightness and distance phenomena (the furtherest mountains on the horizon). Here are ongoing topics for research in phenomenologic astronomy.

Everything self-bright within the terrestrial realm exhibits characteristics approaching sky brightness. Initially, we think of fire and glowing coals, e.g., in torches, candles and gas lamps. Self-bright surfaces, as much as the bodies and lamps which are formed by them, cannot simply be grasped and in general set down, because of their heat. Unlike usual objects, we cannot freely stash them away in order to have them available to bring out later at will. They are not things, but processes which work out from them; all fire is linked together with the air supply and waste air in the whole environment. It cannot continue to burn under a bell jar. In this interconnection to the whole, self-bright bodies become an image of heavenly brightness which always forms a whole, though unceasingly changing. These are not completely reckoned to be among earthly objects. An electric light is not something separate: It depends on the power cord and, also, a generator must be running.

When the great, unified brightness of the heavens shines forth at sunrise, this process carries the entire earth with it: Thousands of different colors and differently oriented surfaces of the earthly realms are joined to the unity of the sky. Daybreak is fulfilled above as below, unstoppable and immense above, differentiated and individualized in the objects below. Nevertheless, they are both part of the panorama surrounding the human being standing below; they cannot occur separately. So, in vision we experience that sun and earth are not separate worlds—as if some kind of light were orbiting a slag-ball in space, which only comes into connection as it allows light rays to be reflected from its exterior. The relationship is most exactly understood as one of self-bright to co-bright: Fire, as a phenomenon of vision, extends itself insofar as surfaces connected to it become visible. Co-bright objects become a part of the fire process, without our needing the hypothetical streaming of invisible light rays. The way such surfaces belong together with their central light is a small image of how, on a larger scale, the sky belongs together with the earth.

We also find the hierarchy again in fire: Many things less bright are linked together with something very bright. And the cause of these many co-bright surfaces ranged about the brightest one is not the light outstreaming from the latter, but simply its presence. Better expressed: as the condition, not the cause. That the fire exists, e.g., is not yet extinguished by water, is the condition that allows the (co-bright) glow of the fire to be seen. Instead of concocting a material causal-chain, we thoughtfully consider the conditions associated with illumination. The condition that enables a surface to be bright is just that, looking out from it, we can see brightness.

If we order these relationships into a brightness series, after sky brightness—and its earthly representative self-bright—in any case still distant in principle from earth, next would come transparent surfaces. Air (to the extent that it is tangible), water and glass can be mentioned here.

After that comes translucency: clouds and leaves. Translucent surfaces have a brightness not connected with the related cupola on the viewed side, but with the cupola on the opposite side. When I view a bright leaf from below, its cupola on this side is the dark earth; so it should be dark. However, the cupola of the sky, above the leaf, is the bright heavens—and the brightness of the [underside of the] leaf is connected to that one. Translucency determines the appearance of the plant-clothed earth and shows powerfully its inner green. Needles, in contrast to leaves, have a matte, often dark [opaque] green; they are not translucent but co-dark with the dark earth (aside from the fact that they have a dark body color).

Very often we see the same leaf in various ways: Perhaps left of the main rib is a dark green half, while the right side is a whiter gray-green. Going a few steps further, this bi-coloration suddenly changes sides. But the cupola of each half is constant, is the same one. Also, the halves are not suddenly co-bright or co-dark. So, if we look around we find variations in the cupola, e.g., a dark copse of trees or a bright opening to the surrounding heavens. If the direction of view from the surface out to this spot in the heavens stands symmetrically to my viewing direction, the surface suddenly glistens whitish-bright. It is no longer the entire cupola but particular directions to portions of it which are determinative.

We can speak therefore of directional brightness or darkness. This is the preliminary stage of mirroring, which reveals far distant images. This exhibiting of something distant by a mirror is hinted at by "directional brightness" in that the surface loses its own color and approaches the color of the heavens—in extreme contrast to transparency, whose "color" depends upon the bodily interior (by body interior is meant not the tangible interior substance, but rather the way the inside meets with the cupola, as explained above). If we don't describe directional brightness out of the surrounding relationships (i.e., toward the viewer) but out of objective, tangible qualities, then we should speak of only the reflectivity of the outer surface, of waxy layers [on the leaf]. And, if we want to utilize the light model, then we should speak of reflection. There are many possibilities to choose from, and here we choose to follow one particular path: the phenomenal one, relating to the whole.

While plants exhibit a play between the transparent, directionally bright and co-bright, the solid earth is almost entirely co-bright. As a whole, in contrast to the cosmos, it is the archetypal symbol of co-bright/co-dark. However, if we glance at the entrance to a cave, then as an expression of the earth's interior there appears self-dark. Like self-bright, self-dark leads out of natural life into the extremes, but to the other side: The self-dark is the representative of impenetrable matter, self-bright of the intangible heavens.

1.7 OVERVIEW

One can arrange the basic concepts of a phenomenological science of light into a correlated image between heaven and earth:

Heavenly brightness

Image of the
celestial heights   **Transparent**

Directionally bright

Self-bright
regions   **Co-bright/co-dark**
in free space   varieties of   **Self-dark**
(barely surfaces)   terrestrial   (opening
e.g., "flame surface,"   surfaces   between
etc.   rigid objects)

Image of
earthly depths

1.8 A NOTE ABOUT METHODOLOGY

Looking back, we note how different the concepts worked out here are from traditional ones. Obviously, the students will speak of the light which "comes out" of a projector or "streams in" the window. That generally is sufficient, especially in technical uses, where (not wanting to understand things comprehensively) one ignores effects and lets some pass by. To the degree that she cuts out experiments, even the teacher will take on such a material-technical way of thinking and also calmly allow the students to use it too. However, if one wishes to consider the great light-connections between earth and cosmos and doesn't want mainly to achieve manipulation of nature, but desires to understand and experience it, then the unusual concepts developed here—just because they are unusual—will be of help to constantly trace out anew the light connections in all their manifestations. Thereby, we leave open the question of what light actually is. Thus, the students receive ideas which are not finished, which have no completed framework as do the theoretical models. Rather we pose ideas which transform, fill themselves out right to their roots, and feed on experiences from the world. With this goal, well-supported by the phenomena, we turn aside with the students from conventional concepts (linear raying-out of light, light sources) and consciously experience and work through how co-brightness and transparency interweave with the sun.[7] Thereby we may connect the inner soul possibilities of taking up the reality of the world in a more differentiated, many-sided and active way than is possible with the geometric ray concept. Light is, then, an interweaving of spread-out connections of that which is visible, it is an idea, grasped in spirit—not in some vague "blue haze" but as an inner concept of the connections of light and darkness, worked through and experienced meanwhile with our own senses. In this context we can again say: Light "comes in through the window" since everything inside here stands in a relationship ruled by the heaven's brightness outside the window. If one sees this pure connective nature of light, then one also intimates its kinship with illuminated human thought.

It doesn't depend upon having this latter as an acknowledged idea. Instead it is important that the teacher present not only conventional facts but that he manifests these ideal possibilities himself. Then, with the students, he can initially make preparation for them to base ideas on an inclusive overview of outer perceptions. This obvious connection of concepts and ideas with perceptions must be practiced in the pre-puberty stage so that, later in the 11th and 12th grades, the students are to inwardly long for a critical fashioning of ideas in fields of perception which go far and wide. The certainty of ideas is given initially by the class teacher. Being active with ideas and percepts can already be practiced; later there arises the attempt to win such certainty from their own judgment, since the possibility of such a basis for ideas was experienced earlier.

II. SEEING AND THE SUN

The new concepts developed up to now in planning the curriculum should again be clarified from another viewpoint and be applied to further optical phenomena. Also, several recapitulations can be helpful.

2.1 HOW AND WHY OPTICS?

THE VALUE OF AN EXPERIENTIAL OPTICS: Many great things are related about light throughout history. From the creation story to *Faust* and the Mystery Dramas of Rudolf Steiner (and in *Study of Man*, Lecture 7), there flows a tale of the essential character of light. And a delicate mystery seizes the listener when light is to be unveiled, as though there was a deep chord inwardly resounding at its discovery.

In the first natural science lecture course for teachers, Rudolf Steiner arrived at the conclusion: "We swim in light. ... Something in us swims out into this illuminated space and unites itself with it. However, one need only reflect a bit on the actual, factual situation and we will find a great distinction between this *being-united* with the direct influence of light-filled surroundings and the *being-associated,* which we have as human beings, namely with the warmth conditions of the environment."[8]

Such words stand as an all-encompassing conclusion at the end of a long journey through many considerations. How should we understand them? This "swimming in light" must be understood, not simply acquiesced to. Here we have to do not simply with an air-bath, a light-bath which gives us the feel of swimming in light. Rather it is meant as a kind of conscious "reflection." This reflecting is not a high-sounding theory about light—it is more than a lot of abstract physics (formulas, measurements, models). Fundamentally, it doesn't depend upon uncovering some background there outside, but rather at first penetrating with reasoned thoughts our own experiences and how we live in light; i.e., with thoughts which grasp our own perceptions, our experienced swimming in light, so that we meet the light in our world at a new stage.

The electromagnetic rays of physics, in contrast to this, are fundamentally dark; they can only be formulated without any sort of sensation of brightness. Such concepts do not bring us further than physical technology.[9] In the last analysis, the certainty or proof of rays conceived in such a physical sense follows from the decision to hypothesize a separate, objective world, unperceived, self-existent, in which subject and object [perceptions and conceptions] have an independent existence.[10] Thus, we are able to use the ray concept to work in a way which quantifies and calculates the objectivity which has thus arisen. The human being then seems unnecessary, [supposedly] reacting with subjective sensations to a world which is constituted complete differently; and, above all, her connection to the essential nature of light can no longer be found.

Our investigations, in contrast—and this is developed further in what follows—must be linked to the perceptual experience, until such time as it is dismembered and distanced by objective world models to something merely caused by material objects. We also want to replace the constantly exorcised approximate thinking [*umdenken*], just here, where we are beginning to practice thinking. Only then can the above quote from Steiner be made fruitful.

Light science is truly the training ground for a science which again wishes to be linked to the intentional experience of the human being. Goethe and Steiner, the fathers of such an approach to nature, first and foremost treated themes from physics and especially from light, not mainly historically, but experimentally, starting from the phenomena!

A proper science of light is a fundamental training for all subsequent quests for knowledge. Dr. Steiner expressed this in discussing the teaching in grade 12: "Optics is very important, since in the spirit-life the individual parts are very much connected together…Why is no real theory of knowledge achieved just there? Because, since Berkeley wrote his book on vision, nothing further which was correct has penetrated vision with knowledge." It also is not a matter of mythical quanta beyond the essence of light, but rather is a matter of a light science as a method for right here! We are seeking a hypothesis-free light science of actual seeing: as a prototype of a phenomenological (Goethean) science which is justified from the point of view of epistemology [theory of knowledge].

2.2 SEEING (VISION) AND WILL

In using the term "knowing," we don't mean a forced mirroring of the existing world we think about, but a recognition of nature in the art of thinking that is a free human deed. Only insofar as we learn to observe what we do are we able to generally differentiate our methods of knowing.

Vision is considered in this sense. We don't ask initially about brightness conditions around the seen objects; rather, we ask about our own intentionality (willed attention) in vision, i.e., how this will activity brings forth vision and transforms it. Thereby lenses and ray-constructions for the eye initially don't come into consideration; instead, *we use the eye itself* without knowing anything of the eye as an object. In the introductory chapter, "On Physiological Colors," of his *Color Theory*, Steiner notes: "Goethe deals with the eye only insofar as he sees, and not through an explanation of seeing from various observations which can be made on a dead eye."[11] We follow Goethe's lead in this respect. Simultaneously, I wish to note that we are active in the act of perception. For perception is not of value as a passive process, whereby stimuli or information *mechanically work their way inward, but perception is a process created by embodied, active will.*[12]

So, in our introduction to vision, we can put first the meeting with sunrise: the transition from deep night to bright, colored day. Feeling our way through pitch-darkness in a cellar to the distant glimmer of light, and then to the gradually increasing brightness of a light bulb in a dark room may serve as a substitute in the classroom. In total darkness, our experience of orienting ourselves to our surroundings is entirely different. By touch we find out the true proportions of things only with difficulty: A table seems endlessly long in one direction. Distant sounds hold us prisoner. Menacing thoughts are hard to overcome, and clearheaded thinking becomes sporadic. We greet the dim brightness in the distance with longing as the first solid and persistent point of orientation. And a strand of light, a candle, establishes a region to which my attention is immediately drawn, toward which I press, in order to establish myself there. For there, out of the two-dimensional outlines of my surroundings is the first gray dawning of a tiny world wherein I can look about with certainty and orient myself. Now I can order the bright surfaces into position with each other, since I now can apprehend objects which have boundaries. And the colors give nourishment to my soul. In the sun-illumined world, I finally feel myself altogether sure, completely objective.

Our understanding of this proper way of seeing various brightly illuminated surfaces can now be augmented by also recognizing the contribution our movement sense makes to vision. The "cross-eye" movement (directing the axes of sight together), "squeezing" (focusing/accommodation) as much as "eye-rolling" (tracing the edges of a form) through movement, grants a terminus for our sense of existence by connecting the vision sense to the movement sense. I know myself as surrounded by objects: They are located there, where my vision "traces" out their positions, as if with an invisible limb. Two things precede such a conclusion of objectivity:

- The delicate musculature of fixation is active in eye-rolling, eye-crossing, and focusing; will acts in a bodily observable form.
- Our visual attention is inwardly guided in fixating on that portion of the field of view which we wish to look at; ensouled will is guided by feelings, wishes, intentions.

This fixating activity is certainly willed, but nowadays is ordinarily neither consciously brought about nor experienced. To the attention activity of fixating is added a comprehending experience of identifying or concluding what it is we are seeing, also willed and self-directed. This ordinary behavior—which will change someday—brings about two results:

- My I-consciousness becomes clear-headed and unbroken since I constantly carry on anew this soul activity of concluding. The normal eye constantly looks about freely. My clear-headed day consciousness creates this as a pleasant, filled-out activity in me.
- My soul experience receives rich contents through the very manifold objects I see, which are constantly around me (in contrast to hearing). This content, however, leaves me free; it never overpowers (i.e., like a strange sound). We have fulfillment and distancing at the same time.

How is it I realize that I am seeing (not hearing or dreaming)? Never by means of the pure contents of perception, but only by a connective soul activity as is sketched out here. The conclusion of objectiveness in space (and organizing things in the space around me, simultaneously given with it) which I become aware of in thought, is the contents of a delicate mental activity with which I direct my perceptual intentionality and fashion it into a content; this activity indicates to me that I have a visual content, that these contents are given perceptually and, certainly, given to me. Thus, I feel: I see.If we work through such aspects of seeing, we can "see" two things:

- The conclusion nowadays that perceptions are "caused" by objects is a habit of consciousness, which happens by itself (in this "age of the consciousness soul," since approximately 1413).
- However, this conclusion is of our own doing and is not an integral component of the content of perceptions.

If we want to connect to the perceptions themselves, first we must also put aside incessantly identifying objective "parts" of the world. For we must first be clear in ourselves. However, that does not usually happen. It can only be intentionally created, never given externally by abundant abstraction on the one hand, nor brought about automatically by objects of perception on the other.

2.3 THE PERIPHERY (SURROUNDINGS) AND SINGLE POINTS; LANDSCAPE

In accord with such distinctions, the path is now clear to rediscover a lost art of seeing: peripheral seeing. We make use of the entire visual field of both our eyes as far as it extends left and right, up and down. If we intentionally surrender ourselves for a moment to this view, we notice that rolling, tightening the lens, and crossing the axes of sight (as we have already indicated for a fixed gaze) remain activities of which we are unconscious. Similarly, the concluding of objectivity fades and we experience quite strongly the concordance of brightness and the confluence of colors: *We experience an environment of brightness and color as a whole.* The feeling of well-being and recuperation arising from a walk outdoors depends greatly on the fact that there are such wholes (fields, forest, sky). Of course we scan the peripheral sectors one after the other using a fixed seeing, but the overall impressions of *peripheral sight* are available without this, and is more than a sum of the individual objects seen fixedly. It has its own quality which constantly works delicately on our living senses. This whole surroundings is at rest; at least it is not willfully moved, like a motor car. It leads to a less mental, more vegetative life and builds up life forces; in contrast, *fixed seeing* engenders forces of consciousness and demolishes life forces. The teacher is already utilizing such a peripheral seeing, for example, when she attends to the experience of the whole class with her feeling.

If one establishes the outer conditions which go together with the brightness of a particularly oriented surface, then to our surprise, we notice that there is actually no such thing as a fixed seeing, separate from the influence of the surroundings. A co-bright surface is bright in dark surroundings, and in dark ones it is bright; the sensation of brightness does not occur without the surroundings exerting a delicate influence. If we look at something through a paper tube blackened inside (in order to exclude the surroundings), the tube acts as the environment: The surface in question appears brighter and therefore spurious.

Individual "pieces" of brightness are constantly in a delicate relationship to the surroundings; they do not occur as completely isolated things, separate from the world. There is no such thing as a surface with a brightness independent of its surroundings. The brightness is not something like area in square inches or the mass of the body. In this we notice a kind of equalization, as in after-images: If we come out of the dark, then a moderate brightness seems brighter than when we come to it out of brighter surroundings into less bright. Therefore a medium bright surface "is" just as bright as it is seen here and now. For in order to arrive at reality, we want to start out from the perception, and that alone can be our constant reality along the way. (Additional phenomena of simultaneous and successive contrast and of "irradiation" are described in Goethe's Color Theory.)

If we take as real what is truly seen—and that is at least pedagogically correct—then in the sense of what has already been portrayed, we can recognize that all bright and dark surfaces of our surroundings constantly form relationships and an inconspicuous whole, which makes up the changes in time of day. The study of the state of affairs throughout the day is a difficult subject, however. Therefore, in teaching we work next toward understanding the conditions under which we ourselves alter surface brightness, e.g., when we cast shadows or introduce a light. We do not seek only references in atmospheric optics but also in experimental manipulations. Therewith we forsake—actually too early—the light studies of nature and, as is advantageous for a concentrated study, begin to experiment. What we treat in the beginning is conventionally termed "radiation of light."

Conventionally such study begins with "light sources." Both of these terms arise, however, out of an intellectually established model of light—as much as from the current meaning with the use of the word *light*. Therefore, we will totally avoid them at first. For then one may hope to express the phenomena purely and thereby lead to a meaningful impression. And only afterward will we look into the encroaching ideas.

2.4 ROLE OF THE SENSES

The sense impressions of lightness and darkness and those of color must be combined—as with acoustics—with the perceptions of other senses. Thereby in our thinking they will achieve the form of outer reality which enables us to speak of things existing there outside. Over the centuries we have unconsciously come to the point where only this activity of fixing on outer objects is called physics. Thereby the activity itself is not seen, but only its results—the materially conceived objectivity. Then this is taken as a cause (as we will show with examples), as the source of reality in perceptions. We have twofold:

- The relation of seeing to other senses [e.g., self-movement, balance]
- With our thinking activity, we construe a causative objectivity, presumed as basis.

We cannot take part uncritically in the second unconscious step (referring all causes into objects), for it is an illusion we have created: Its contents (e.g., the object) are viewed as the initial reality and not as something realized within, through our own activity of forming ideas (which is correct). However, the first step, the connection to other senses, is absolutely necessary from the beginning. Only it must be a connection to actual perceptions, not already to conclusions about objectivity, or to mental concepts arising out of the second step. The conventional understanding of light falls into this mistake, taking light to be a quasi-material stream, raying out from a light source and finally even measuring this spreading out in terms of mechanical velocity. Such unexamined mental conceptions have piled up the greatest obstacles to our pedagogical goal.

Every cluster of sense experiences of light and color are initially experiences of the senses of movement and balance, insofar as we say: There is light, or there that is dark. Between the two indicated locales is a nook of space within which I turn myself to and fro (self-movement). The direction to the indicated place stands in a definite balance or laterality relative to my erect stance (sense of balance, which is experienced meanwhile). The immediate use of ray drawings (casting shadows, mirroring, etc.) would be abstract. For the linearity used in such drawings arises as an abstraction from the movement sense—linked to it but greatly abstracted and stripped of perceptual experiences. Moreover, such diagrams are never drawn from the viewpoint of the observer but from an onlooker's position. The ray diagrams lead away from the individual's actual experience.

2.5 THE COSMIC SURROUNDINGS

Just as in acoustics we met music as a higher unity of tone as its real occurrence which the human being shapes toward higher goals, so in optics, the real connection of light and dark with the cosmic organism is met in the changes of day and night, the course of the sun. It permeates completely all dominions of nature and our active human life. What was a cultural process in acoustics, in optics is an all-encompassing unifying process of the earth. It stands over against the earthly-dark, the individualizing through earthly mass, mechanics. Also in optics, nature is not born out of art but out of the cosmos, though not yet an objective part of earthly material.

Thereby the actual basis of optics (the sun, the light of the sky) becomes somewhat unbounded, calls upon an ever higher, unknown struggle of our understanding—and still remains clearly concrete (day and night, solar time, season). This striving toward something higher which yet remains mysterious gives the teaching its worth, its humanity. In acoustics it is music that helps us toward this; in light science it is the periphery of the cosmos. Even in experiments in a closed room we experience this principle of the periphery.

Light science is a study of the sun. This is a real challenge. We live so deeply embedded in its unified, encompassing activity that at first we cannot present the students with anything differentiated or diverse. Why has this great phenomenon of the sun become so inaccessible to rational thinking? This is due to the development of the modern worldview, which presents the sun as a body out there, about which other bodies circle, from random initial positions, guided only by blind gravity—the sun as an inaccessible gas-ball in empty space.

It is an entirely different thought (the above were only thoughts!) to open the gate to the sun. As a beginning we can say: In general the sun is wherever it acts. And, stronger, we live within the sun, in its creation of brightness and in our daily rhythms. Here it surrounds, it holds us. That outer orb is only the external aspect, a distant symbol of its present, immediate might. Here, next to me, is the activity of the "soft transformation of its day,"[13] not in scientifically calculated movements of a cosmic body outside in space.

Thereby we find ourselves embroiled in the conflict between the geocentric and the heliocentric worldviews. We don't initially focus at all on the orbiting of individual bodies, but instead wish to express our local situation in a hypothesis-free way, certainly in the way we experience it.

The first perceptual experience we investigate with the students could (as already indicated) well be the sunrise; best on a class trip after traveling through the last hours of night. The night is still timeless. With the first graying of morning, the occurrence begins to take effect about us which we can term sun, or time. That the sun processes with sunrise increase to a din is artistically put in *Faust* (Prologue and Ariel Scene). Native peoples report on remnant sound of the sun (Laurens van der Post, *The Heart of the Hunter*).

2.6 SIMULTANEOUS COLOR CONTRAST

After we have found the higher unity in our light studies with sun and earth, i.e., have "come to our senses," we meet a new quality: color. This is given us at the same time in sunrise.

As with all celestial phenomena, the colors never occur unconnected or separately. The pale turquoise and yellow-green answer a penetrating morning-red, tiny spots painted over the other colors on individual clouds. And, afterward, the first blue of morning answers the orange of the sun's disc, still standing low. Only at the point when the darkness is completely overcome are the color changes lost in preference for the uniform, hard blue of the firmament and the shining, inaccessible sun. And as the sun rises, not only over the sky but also over the earth, so also the day reigns here about us. In the manner already described, brightness makes possible our objective consciousness, growth, and freedom; we have the sun. It is not far away; it is the sun-process in us. The disc in the heavens is the distant symbol, the ruling sign of these processes.

A second such sign is the [globe of the] eye. Here again we will not turn to the conventional presentation that light rays pass in from outside and then we see images via our optic nerve. Our approach has to do with our penetrating outside with our activity, actually living outside in active vision.

2.7 AFTER-IMAGES (SUCCESSIVE COLOR CONTRAST)

In order to get to know the eye as an active organ, we now investigate after-images. First we rest our gaze on the crossing point of the window frame and window panes, then switch to a medium-gray surface: The previously dark forms become bright and the bright dark. The eye responds to extremes with an equalizing activity. Alternatively: Quietly gaze at a white carton with a black triangle (or similar clear figure), then snatch it away—keeping the gaze on the same spot. A bright triangle appears on a dark square. Both in looking at the high-contrast scene and in seeing the after-image, it is essential not to try to survey the scene for objects, or to grasp it, but to take in the whole field of view, to linger in the widths of our visual panorama and pay attention to the whole—looking in a way which is more aware of the entirety and less intent on identifying particular objects. To make the after-image more noticeable for those students who have difficulty, we can use colored figures (turquoise blue or green on white).

The after-image effect is well-known but is usually given a place as a trivial curiosity of optics, by which one implies that it is known, but should be considered an illusion. This disdain makes sense as long as we don't try to go beyond merely verifying after-images. But there are two directions by which we can go further.

The first is the presence of will in perception. Conscious activity, the conclusion of objectivity and discreteness, the lasting distinction and tracing of images, all these must be taken as results of either a willed seeing, or an indifferent viewing of after-images. We are considering seeing itself as a deed carried out, and not the variety of objects seen. And if we investigate this using dark, not light-colored scraps, then we will be rewarded with magical, glowing colored after-images: luminous, complementary colors. The externally visible color composition of the morning and evening skies described above, the turquoise-red and blue-orange color pairs appear once again, out of seeing itself.

Aside from a schooling of our willed perception, after-images place yet a second question before us: What actually is expressed in this reversal of brightness which occurs with the creation of complementary colors? When we look at the contrast-poor gray wall after gazing at the cross of the window frame, vision interweaves these two scenes, contrast-rich and contrast-poor, by letting the after-image appear from the latter. The contrast-rich image outshines the monotone image seen behind it. However, the image interwoven with the contrast-poor image of the gray wall is not the image formerly seen, but its light/dark and color reversal. The shapes which are grasped by the movement sense active in vision and not just by seeing, these remain unaltered; it is the brightness and colors of the surfaces which appear changed. This comes with steady, fixed gazing, and already comes to expression in ordinary vision: The bright parts become muted in the blended brightness, and the dark ones become less dark.

This delicate moderation of contrast which at first does not yet have anything to do with the after-image can be directly observed: Slightly shift the gaze to the side and dark spots acquire a bright border. The after-image is already acting over the initial image. This self-arising equalization accompanying a quiet gazing at the initial image is already an interweaving of the light and dark parts: Bright becomes somewhat changed and reversed to dark. In the after-image, we intensify this potential tendency by directing the gaze onto a contrast-poor gray. The previous contrast-moderating activity continues to act; the image against which it worked now disappears; the continuing balancing activity of vision creates a new, reversed complementary image. If one immerses oneself in a saturated green, then one experiences its saturation by unconsciously creating red. Individual colors and individual states of brightness are somewhat unreal; our vision relates everything into a whole.

Repeatedly the question arises: Are after-images real or are they subjective? This is not the right question. Things which are ostensibly subjective nevertheless may have the greatest effect in nature and on the perceiving human being. One can therefore call it actual (active) even if it cannot be described as objective or grasped. And in addition, after-images are never subjective in the sense of being pleasing. They are much more inter-subjective; they exist between observer and observed.

As said earlier, they are not completely objective. They lack the second sense quality (tracing-out, movement sense; see Section 2.4 above). Since we make after-images by focusing on the "prototype" image while holding the gaze fixed and thereby excluding the movement sense, we are led into a visual impression (the subsequent after-image), which the self-movement sense can no longer take hold of. For the after-image does not allow itself to be traced over or felt out point-wise, since with each shift in the eye's gaze it floats along. To the extent it is deprived of this second sense quality, it doesn't afford the usual focusing on objects existing there outside. We leave behind the distance measurable, the objective realm which otherwise contributes to our consciousness: The after-image accompanies us inescapably and fades against our will.

We ought to leave the subject of after-images in this delicate untouchability. To say, "It stems from the eye" means only the objective conclusion of a third observer, inserted as a bare judgment because we want to have objectivity at any cost. For a person who attends to the after-image does not notice the organ of the eye, but experiences only the act of seeing.

The color laws of after-images yield Goethe's color wheel. We find an ordering of the cold and warm colors. Now, we can study where the warm colors characteristically occur in nature: in blood, in fire. Here many things can be connected. Here also, we can call forth a feeling of what the being of color means chiefly, as we consider first the gray, white, and black, and then the colored after-images. The experience of color comes to expression very clearly if we travel a path in the dusky morning twilight, along which we later go again in daylight: We are astounded that we didn't see the entirety of beautiful colors the first time. In our mind we can compare nature in black & white and in color. Only with such observations do we truly come to the experience that a new realm is opened for us through color.

III. BRIGHTNESS AND SHADOW

3.1 THE CUPOLA IN CONTRAST TO SURROUNDINGS - A RECAP

In our environment we see surfaces or shapes of various brightness; among these are those whose brightness is surprisingly great, e.g., the sun. Earthly surfaces about us are always bright, if—from their surface outward—we can see something very bright, for example the sun. (see also Section 1.3, Co-brightness) On the other hand, it clearly does not matter for their brightness if their surroundings are bright from our point of view. We can do the following experiment:

A candle flame is placed in front of the bright window and its brightness is observed. Then, compare its brightness in a darkened room. Immediately it is evident that its brightness depends upon the surroundings, and the reverse is certainly true: If the surroundings are bright, the candle seems dim. (compare variations of Op 7)

We can recall the principle of equalization discussed earlier in connection with after-images. We ought to avoid the abstract notion that a candle has a particular brightness, like a measurable thing independent of all surroundings, and only appears different in each environment. That is not the reality we experience, and it is nonsensical, since we never see a candle without a surrounding. Visible things are only perceptible in the environment of other visible things.

Consider the experiment with the white globe (Op 3): If we stand in the middle of the classroom with an egg, it can be seen clearly that the window half is bright, and in contrast the other half is dark. This experiment is moderately independent of the background seen simultaneously. If, for example, a light bulb is positioned in the space behind the students, the division of brightness on the egg will be dramatically altered, although the backdrop seen by the students next to the egg is relatively same; the lamp is located behind them and, in viewing the egg, is not visible. Any variations of brightness on the egg depend on whether— with my eye at the surface of the egg looking back toward the onlookers—I can see some new brightness. The egg is always bright where its surface is oriented to other brightnesses, and the side of the egg which is oriented away from brightness is dark. The surface brightness of the egg, in the sense of the previously described influence of the surroundings, is not dependent only on what can be seen around it (the backdrop), but mainly on what can be seen looking from the egg outward, and is often invisible, behind the observer. Thus, we find the fundamental rule:

Every surface in the world is just as bright as (from its location outward) we can see a general brightness in a cupola (hemisphere) which we see into looking out from the surface in question.

A surface which relates in this way to its cupola we termed "co-bright"; and a body bounded by such surfaces is a co-bright body. We distinguish between the backdrop and the cupola: the visible half-sphere seen from the surface outward, seen from the body bearing the surfaces—with an eye located at the surface in question. The observer and his surroundings are considered from the viewpoint of the surface, including the cupola right up to the surface's horizon. For a level surface, this horizon is easily described: It is the earthly horizon. In connection to this we have done the experiment with a white tablecloth and a light bulb, held at a constant distance, and moved stepwise from the zenith to below the horizon (Op 2). Just before the "setting" of the bulb, when we reach the diagonal position, the orientation of the surface to the bulb is very oblique and the surface becomes dark; imagine the horizon of an obliquely inclined surface and its diagonally oriented cupola.

Now, we examine the brightness of a candle placed in front of the classroom, with additional candles set up nearby but concealed from the observers (Op 7). We observe that its brightness, when it is in front of a similar backdrop, is not dependent on the other candles which are not seen but in the cupola of the seen candle. We find the following rule:

A surface whose brightness depends only (moderately) on the backdrop seen with it, but not on other bright surfaces present in its cupola, such a surface we term "self-bright."

A body which possesses such *cupola-independent surfaces* we call a *self-bright body,* e.g., a lamp. Thereby we arrive at a synonym for the conventional (but avoided) expression "light source." Our self-bright is not based on the outstreaming of an invisible light, whose rays prick through, but is explained by means of the relationships with the surroundings and what is visible about it, which we could see by turning around. That a candle flame is something self-bright is indicated by the fact that it is used to brighten a dark cellar. If it went along with the brightness in its cupola, i.e., with the dark cellar walls, then the further it passes into the cellar and the more dark it is, the darker it should become. We recognize self-bright surfaces usually already without putting something black into their cupolas or having to move to where it is dark. If one goes to the location of the surface in question, and can see no brighter surfaces in the cupola (all visible surfaces are far darker), then the bright-appearing surface can only be self-bright. Naturally, self-bright surfaces generally cast an effect out into their surroundings, and actually cannot exist separate from their surroundings. We recall the sky's brightness or fire, which constantly must be open to the environment. A strong departure from this basic principle is presented by electrically lighted bodies. However, even they cannot function without a connection to the environment, at least for a time (batteries need to be charged, connection wire installed, etc.).

As a contrast to this variable, flickering, substance-consuming self-bright, we show a cardboard box, thickly covered and completely dark inside, with a thumbnail-size opening cut in its face (Op 6). The surface appears as paper with a small dark spot in the middle: the hole. The opening seems at the same time to be a part of the surface. If we go around in the room with this "holed" surface, orienting it to the bright heavens, to a dark corner, to a candle flame or a lamp, it never appears differently than black. Such a cavity is no longer co-bright, but totally separated from the environs and always dark: We term it "self-dark." It is a deepest black, darker than a black cloth, crepe paper or anything else.

3.2 AN ORDERING OF NATURE

We have now three descriptions: the self-bright, the co-bright (co-dark) and the self-dark. Thereby an overall organization of nature is manifest:

- The *self-bright* which has its source in the open heavens into which we gaze looking upward. Its archetypal symbol is the sun. Constant movement and greatest openness describes self-bright.
- The archetypal image of the *co-bright* is the earth's surface, toward which we look downward, upon which we stand, and which accompanies the changing brightness and color of the sky.
- The archetype of the *self-dark* is the opening into the earth, the caves and underworld beneath the surface of the earth.

In sky and earth we can survey the extremes: the heavenly bright, which is never dependent on other brightness in its surroundings but presents a bright surrounding for other things; the earthly dark, which also is independent of its surroundings, since it has fallen out of connection with it and now lies in the midst of earthly heaviness.

Within these three principles, we find the greatest differentiation in the realm of the co-bright. Every earthly surface, each object in nature has its own, distinct capacity for co-brightness. Thus the great multiplicity of kinds of surfaces already comes to expression in the earth's surface as well as in the visible objects. Co-bright now differentiates itself in the entirely new realm of colors (earth colors).

The greatest capacity for co-brightness is possessed by white. The cross-country skier orients herself by minute differences in brightness, which indicate the angle of the snow surface to her, since the brightness sensitively expresses how the snow accompanies different cupolas. In black snow it is difficult to travel without danger in polar twilight. Color is a child of the meeting of heavenly brightness and earthly darkness. It occurs even in the sky when bright and dark meet as distinct entities in evening's or morning's glow.

3.3 SHADOWS

We set up perhaps a half dozen candles at the front of a darkened classroom (Op 8). Each is placed inside a white cylinder of translucent paper (tracing paper). We turn around now and look at the rear portion of the classroom, and we see swimming, flickering shadows, i.e., a mostly diffuse transition from brighter and darker regions. Only when we take the candles out from inside their paper shades (and finally also reduce their number) do we then achieve sharper shadows. Thereby, we can already express it thus: The scene with sharp contrast, very bright within very dark surroundings (candle[s] in front of the dark table), when we turn about, produces a definite, similar contrast behind us between bright and darker regions: the shadows [i.e., noticeable borders to the light/dark regions]. A more generally spread-out brightness produces a diffuse shadow scene when we turn around.

SHADOW DARKNESS

On what does the depth or darkness of the shadows depend? With a cardboard box and two lamps mounted on a board (Op 9), we fashion two different self-bright bodies. One consists of a lamp placed inside a milk-glass globe. The second is made by another lamp inside a cardboard carton, with a large round hole cut in its larger side (the same diameter as the glass globe) covered with onion-skin paper (any translucent paper), making a body which is self-bright on only one side. With various wattage light bulbs, probably also with a varistat (variable transformer), we set these up in the front of the classroom (with the carton lamp appropriately directed) so that the rear wall is made equally bright using either one. The carton lamp leaves the front classroom wall in darkness, in contrast to the globe lamp. With the carton lamp, the shadows in back are darker.

Also, if we look forward from the students' position toward the carton lamp, we see a moderately strong contrast between the bright disc and the surrounding darkness of the front space and wall. Turning around, we see bright areas with a correspondingly strong contrast to dark shadows. The contrasts on front and rear walls are both altered together with the globe lamp; now, it is bright about the lamp in front and the shadows in the rear are less deep. Thus, for every kind of lamp, we find that the contrast we see in the scene in front corresponds to the contrast of the shadow scene in back.

Incorporating all these observations, we can think of the lighting in this case as actually much larger than the disc of the globe: It is the whole front area. The self-bright spot for the rear (shadowed) wall's cupola is no longer just the bounded body (disc of the globe in front); it is the entirety of all the bodies and surfaces involved. In brightness terms, it is a whole region of space. If we place a paper tube (blackened inside) in front of the carton lamp, oriented so that it forms an equally bright co-bright region on the rear wall as before, the shadows there become darker still.

Then the question arises: For the surrounding (co-dark) regions (which we take to be shadows), upon what surfaces in the surroundings do they depend in brightness? With the foundational idea that bright orients itself to brightness, and dark to darkness, we soon realize that the "shadow" areas depend on everything which can be seen in front except for the lamp itself, since the lamp cannot be seen from the location of the shadows. As for every other surface, shadow surfaces depend upon their cupola which would be seen looking out from their location. But, for the shadow regions, it is just the self-bright disc their cupolas lack. The shadows form an image of the darkness which surrounds the self-bright disc. Thereby we distinguish the shadows from the back side of the shadow-casting bodies which are not oriented to the self-bright disc, and are dark because they are turned away from it. The dark back sides are oriented not to the bright surfaces about the self-bright disc in front, but to the opposite or rear of the room, the shadow scene. The term "self-shadowed," often used for the back side of these shadow-casting bodies, is therefore confusing; for, in the sense of the cupola concept, it has nothing to do with "shadowing" that their rear surfaces are dark. Rather, it is a matter of their orientation to the dark rear wall forming a darkness in their cupola. So, dark-oriented might be better.

SHADOW ALIGNMENT

In the foregoing, we have connected the perceptions of bright-dark to the individual's turning front and back, and also to the facing-toward and facing-away of surfaces. In this way, the sensations of sight were intertwined with our sense of movement and our sense of self-balance (with our facing-toward and facing-away). This link with the movement sense can be strengthened through a particular demonstration. We place several stools behind each other, so that, upon moving our head, from the rear stool they all disappear behind the first one. The visible edges are, so-to-say, "straight behind" one another. The observer just faces the seen tableau and cannot judge what this alignment means, other than as a planar image. Only when one *moves* in space (across the row of stools) does the abstract judgment that they are "in a straight line" arise out of that movement and our movement sense. Another (third) person, who has not walked along the row of stools, but looks down the row as along a taut cord, will also come to the conclusion "in alignment."[14]

Only by the process of movement followed by the sense of movement do we also pass from seeing the "visible alignment" (seen as simultaneous disappearance) to the concept "linearity." Since shadow formation has to do with the *alignment* of bright/dark boundaries of the shadowed scene with where one can or cannot see the self-bright around the shadowed surface, this (concept) "in alignment" comes into consideration overlaid on the (perception) "alignment in line of sight." If we put a surface behind the shadow-casting object, and move it toward the object's dark back side, then we constantly get shadows on the surface. The location of the shadow-edge during this movement describes straight lines, raying out from the casting object's edge; the shadows are present in space, even if not made visible by some surface there.

With this we could construe shadows as made of straight lines; but this would be abstract, since a point-sized, self-bright spot of light is not the usual case. In reality shadow sharpness and shadow intensity always alter with the distance from the shadowing body. A shadowed surface "sees" the self-bright disc as larger in its cupola (relative to the shadowing body) the closer the bright disc is (distance from the shadow-casting to shadowed surface being constant); so, the shadows are less sharp for a close-up light, since a side-to-side motion of our eyes makes less difference (it doesn't cross as sharp a transition). Only in conventional geometrical drawing do the potential light and dark boundaries lie along rays of straight lines. We should not speak of a homogeneous shadow space behind the object, since the phenomenon is only a potential: If we hold a surface behind it, the shadows would be visible (manifesting the relative depth and sharpness of the shadow); so, the lines are not real but potential lines, idealized lines formed by the relationships of unplanned, potential bright/dark boundaries. The potential lines can all be realized together only by means of smoke filling a region of space; but then the contrast is poorer, due to the smoke. The full contrast value of bright/dark boundaries remains only potential except for the one place it is realized (where we have the paper). Those ray-like bright regions seen in a slight haze beneath clouds, as streaks which point to the sun, have nothing to do with light rays which stream down. The sun imprints the space with a clear signature. This signature remains stable and is oriented to the sun. The whole space points to the sun, not because something streams out from it, but the shafts are places from which the sun is visible, and these bright regions of atmospheric space are made visible by atmospheric mist (not by the sun). Everything visible will usually be oriented to the sun as the brightest.

SHADOW SHARPNESS

With our shadow studies, we are led from the outset to see that shadows can be more or less distinct. With various experiments we can show that large, self-bright surfaces, e.g., a large cutout in a carton, covered with rice paper, produces very indistinct shadows. The smaller the self-bright disc, the sharper the shadows. If we make the disc even smaller, by using a very small, very bright lamp (e.g., a halogen lamp from a projector) directed onto the lab table, then we achieve uncomfortably sharp shadows, the like of which is never seen on the open earth under the sky (Op 10). Along with all this we can comment that often one has to get sufficiently far from the shadowing surface in order to avoid being in a position in which we cannot see the large self-bright surface (disc), to where we can see the whole. The eye must move very far from the shadowed surface, diagonally from the bright/dark boundary, in order to make the self-bright surfaces become visible. According to our basic statement (Section 3.1), a surface is just as bright as the brightness we can see from its surface outward. If one sees only half of the lamp, then it is only half as bright there; if one sees the whole lamp, it must be completely bright.

The production of a series of interconnected drawings in experiment Op 10 is a training for a thinking which creates out of perceptions and out of the lower senses also (through holistic seeing). Contrast this to the schooling of the intellect, which starts out using the lower senses in mere abstractions of geometric ray diagrams. In addition, we can observe that shadows which are proportionally nearer the shadowing body (relative to the overall distance to the light) are sharper than shadows that we find further away. This shows up very well with the sun, which makes a tree, bush, blade of grass or garden fence cast shadows: The shadows of the trunk and the lower branches are sharp, higher up they dissolve, and the network of leaves at the crown shows a tendency to form round, dark and bright light splotches. (see Grade 7, Section IV-1)

With this phenomenon, we understand something of the nature of the shadow. In physics, shadows are usually cast onto a surface which is totally flat, exactly transverse, and, above all, especially white. However, this never occurs in nature: Shadows constantly fall on something else, on surfaces which already manifest an appearance, which are differentiated. One also has the experience that in the shadows cast on an object, the image of another object appears. And since the surface on which the shadow is visible often lies diagonally, and is irregular (non-planar), the image of the shadow-casting object is immediately interwoven with the form of the shadowed object—changed into a new image which says something about both. In this we meet again the interweaving activity of light: As soon as the sun stands over a landscape, all individual objects are interwoven, insofar as they stand near to each other. The entire landscape is thereby imprinted with a uniform directionality of the sun. In their boundary sharpness, the shadows become an image of the distance between objects. The shadows of narrow objects or high-flying birds are lost at greater distances and are no longer visible. This interweaving aspect of light is able to affect only large, massive objects at great distances; the tiny ones are entirely dissolved. A very concrete feature of this interweaving activity is expressed in the sunlit landscape, as objects are set free of their isolation.

3.4 WHAT IS LIGHT?

By going through all these phenomena, for us light becomes a force which allows us to *consciously grasp the connections* within the world and nature and the manifold way everything unites with everything else. And every surface is part of the cupola of innumerable other surfaces, which again are part of its cupola. This all-encompassing unifying activity is depicted by Novalis for example in his glorification of light in the Hymn of the Night. However, it is not totally free of a quasi-physical idea of light. In the first verse, he presumes a space (this idea arises through the connection of brightness), and he stirs up the light theory of his time with "rays and waves"; rays of the corpuscular theory of Newton, waves of the wave theory of Huygens. Anyhow, we should not (mis)understand it in this way.

Each surface is connected to all others, and naturally this is especially true for self-bright surfaces in the cupola of other surfaces. The self-bright surfaces create a hierarchical dominance, which again connects a self-bright body to various other surfaces. We should not draw a causal chain from the self-bright body to the co-bright bodies, presuming light somehow invisibly whizzing along. Rather the causality is only this: If I place the self-bright body so that another surface is turned toward it, that surface becomes simultaneously bright. It is not possible to have a self-bright body without the surrounding surfaces oriented to it also becoming bright (speed of light considerations are neglected here). The source of becoming bright is the orientation of surfaces to the self-bright, not the "light" streaming out of it. Perhaps, better than "source" we can say "condition." A mediator in between (the "light rays") is a hypothesis.

This is already a characteristic feature of brightness: It establishes a connection, which directly grasps everything that is visible from its location, without mediating causes in between. *The idea of such connections can be termed "light."* As soon as the bodies are densely packed upon each other, there is no longer a light connection. For example, holding a sheet of paper parallel over the table and lowering it, the shadow becomes increasingly sharp and dark. At the instant of touchdown, the shadow has the exact form of the paper silhouette and is deep black. Now it is neither an expression of the form and size of the lamp, nor of the brightness of its surroundings, nor of the placement of shadower and shadowed relative to the direction to the lamp; the shadow falls out of all the weaving connections. Now it is only an impression of the material object, it falls out of "light." To that extent we can say, no light comes any more between the paper and the table. "No light" then means no connectiveness, no interweaving images with something distant in the light space (the connective space).

To the extent that light is a connecting essence of such a sort, it possesses a certain kinship with our conscious thinking activity. Out of this it is understandable that the activity of making-bright (illumination) previously discussed can take place in our conscious activity. Light is not a quasi-physical something which somehow spreads itself out. Rather light is an Idea which arises out of human observing and thinking, an idea of the connections of brightness phenomena. Space arose with light in the Old Sun stage of cosmic evolution (*Occult Science, an Outline*, R. Steiner).

Experiments in Optics

LIGHT & DARKNESS

OP 1A DARKNESS RECEDES (SUNRISE)

Mount a bicycle bulb (6-volt, 3-watt) in a socket, connected to a variable power-pack (varistat) and gradually energized. Surround the bulb with a paper cylinder, in order not to see the lamp but to observe the brightness of the dawning glow on the ceiling and front wall. One can also improvise the experiment with a refrigerator bulb or sewing-machine lamp using a variable resistance or powerstat. An ordinary dimmer usually won't go low enough—the lamp does not get totally dark. After brightening this small bulb, turn a stronger lamp bright, most effectively a 1000-watt quartz-halogen bulb [see outdoor yard lights in hardware shop]. If our 30-volt/30-amp power-pack is used, switch off the 6-volt socket, set the voltage control on zero and then insert the large lamp. Experience the stages: (1) pitch darkness; (2) first glimmer; (3) eastern glow; (4) twilight; (5) sun illumined, (6) colored daylight illuminating objects (set up previously in the front). First comes illumination ("dawn"), then the sun is visible. Question: What is "radiance" or "glory"?

OP 1B LANDSCAPE SHADOWS?

Examine the orientation of shadows on an outside landscape by drawing the shadows around several vertical objects. All the shadows are unified by the sun.

OP 1C AFTER-IMAGES: THE ACTIVE EYE

Investigate what we see after gazing fixedly at a window frame (a scene with strong contrast) for 60 seconds, then turning away and gazing at a uniform gray surface. Note how the after-image is the same shape, but light-dark is reversed. Note how it floats, unwilled, along with our gaze; it is not a usual object of vision. [Also, note how the after-image metamorphoses; note how it reverses again to a positive if viewed against something bright—e.g., the closed eyelids turned toward the sun!]

Our active vision sense always strives to maintain a balance. When we are filled with one color, our vision sense presents the complementary color. Next, explore the behavior of vision in colored scenes: The green grass and the blue sky are answered by a reddish-purple and by an orange-red. Pale initial colors produce the strongest (deepest) complementary after-image colors.

OP 2 HORIZON AND CUPOLA (ANGLE OF ILLUMINATION)

To introduce the **dependence of surfaces on their surroundings**:

A   Observe the influence of colored clothing on a sheet of white paper laid flat on the table. [The sheet "takes up" the brightness and even the color of adjacent surfaces.]

B   Cover a card table with a cloth as free of folds as possible. Using a 2-meter (6 ft) tall stand which has a 1000-watt quartz lamp (yard lamp) attached to a stand, position the lamp directly over the table: The white cloth is now pure bright. Now incline the lab stand at various angles while keeping the lamp the same distance away from the table top; the table is no longer perpendicular to the lamp. Each movement of the lamp to a new orientation alters the brightness: The more diagonal the lamp, the darker the table.

Note: Distinguish observing the surface or scene from observing from the surface outward (the cupola). If we pass below the plane of the surface, it suddenly becomes dark and further movement has hardly any further effect. The lamp has "set" for this surface. Mark this lamp height on the wall (with masking tape). Now, repeat the setting experiment in other directions, marking other walls. The circle connecting all similar marks is the "horizon" of the [table] top; it is naturally an extension of its surface.

The teacher could also illuminate various solids (e.g., polyhedra) and note the brightness differences. Examine watermarked paper under strong sidelight.

OP 3 ILLUMINATION SENSOR OR ALL-SEEING GLOBE

Paint a large Florence (round-bottomed) flask or a 9-inch milk-glass lamp globe very evenly with flat white house paint (or spray paint). If necessary, make it matte using fine sandpaper. This globe is now a kind of reflector of the brightness in the whole environment—one can move it about like a probe or sensor, using it to reveal these brightness conditions.

OP 4 TENT; CARTON-GROTTO

In lieu of the lamp stand over a tablecloth, a grotto can be constructed from a carton painted black inside. Place the sensor-globe inside and observe the way it shows the dark area we created in its cupola.

SELF-LUMINOUS (BRIGHT) BODIES

OP 5 SELF-BRIGHTNESS

Prepare a candle-shaped light bulb (long and thin) in a socket mounted vertically on a board. The second globe inverted over it ought to completely cover the socket, and the light bulb should penetrate into the globe. A 9-inch porch light globe works well. Conceal the electrical cord with a cloth or empty tin can. The concealed dimmer [or varistat] is turned brighter so slowly that we first discern only a yellowing of the globe, and then later an illumination of it. Note how its ghostly glow is independent of any light-dark situation which may surround it; its connection to the surrounding is severed.

[Experiment with the "dim glow" globe near a window, near a second lamp, etc. The attached shadow fades with self-brightness.]

OP 6 SELF-DARKNESS

Set up a cardboard box as above, but not too small, at least the size of a side table, and a small hole cut in one face. The aperture should be about thumbnail-size and the edges should not be ragged. When we shine a flashlight on it to see if any brightness can be seen, the hole stays dark. The more the surface of the box is illuminated, the darker the hole is seen to be!

OP 7A SELF-BRIGHT, CANDLE FLAME

Alongside a visible candle we place two more candles right and left on the table, concealed from the students. Observe the brightness of the central candle. Now, blow the flanking candles out; thus, the background behind the central candle becomes darker and the remaining candle flame becomes brighter. If the candle flame were co-bright, it ought to become dimmer with the extinguishing of the other two [as its cupola becomes darker]. Note the difference between cupola, surroundings seen from the surface, and the backdrop, all seen from the observer's viewpoint.

Shaded candles

OP 7B VARIOUS SURFACES IN NATURE

[Explore instances in nature of: self-bright (sun, full moon, flame, lantern); transparent (air, water); translucent (leaves); co-bright (many opaque surfaces); and self-dark surfaces (cavities). – Trans.]

OP 8 SHADOW SCENES

A. In the front of the darkened classroom, set up a half dozen candles, each covered with a cylindrical paper chimney. The students observe their shadows on the rear wall. [A swimming, indistinct shadow scene is visible].

B. Now, (1) with a few of the paper chimneys removed, observe the scene on the wall behind; then (2) with all chimneys removed; then (3) with only a few of the candles burning. [The shadows grow progressively sharper. The shadow contrast (the sharpness of the edge) corresponds to the contrast of the self-bright body, in the cupola of the shadowed surface. Distinguish a bright spot vs. large, diffuse bright area.]

OP 9 SHADOW DARKNESS [CARTONED LAMP/OPEN LAMP]

Fasten two sockets onto a small wood board and furnish with a power cord with a standard plug. It can be plugged onto a dimmer [or a varistat]. Fix the board to the bottom of the cardboard box (from Ops 4 & 6 above). On the larger side cut out a circular window (9-inch or the diameter of the globe) and cover it with translucent paper. Cover the other socket with a milk-glass globe. Turn them on alternately, and investigate which makes the rear wall of the classroom brighter. This one is reduced to match the brightness of the other by inserting a smaller bulb and/or by means of the dimmer [varistat]. This completes the preparation.

The experiment involves using a paper silhouette, chair or other object to create shadows on the rear wall. Compare the shadows created by each lamp. [The carton lamp shadows are darker although the surroundings are equally bright.]

The "boxed" lamp aperture is seen (looking into the cupola from the screen outward) as brightness surrounded by a darker box front. The "open" lamp is seen as bright surrounded by co-bright nearby surfaces, which are carried along with it in brightness, i.e., the contrast around the self-bright lamp reappears in the corresponding shadow's contrast.

Shadow drawings

Light source (paper lantern)

transition zone

heavy shadow zone

Shadow-casting board

View of the student-observer to the wall, toward the light

View from the class: the shadows

OP 10 SHADOW SHARPNESS

Op10A JAPANESE PAPER LANTERN: Using a socket mounted on a board as in the preceding experiment, we cover it with a paper lantern globe. Immediately all shadows in the room become weak and a very cozy environment arises. The lamp is placed to one side of the classroom front. Erect a large surface on the front table (vertically mounted wood board, covered by paper). Immediately behind it a shadow arises. The board is shoved further away from the light; now the shadow is less sharp. Now a student goes to the position of the half shadow on the wall and looks with one eye toward the paper lantern, the other eye closed. Slowly, he shifts position from the unshadowed area to the shadowed area, reporting how much of the Japanese paper lamp he can see. His reports correspond strongly to the strength of shadow we observe on his face. The students can establish the relationship in a series of dual illustrations of the following sort:

Op10B LIGHT BULB: The investigation is repeated with the bare light bulb and no paper lantern. [The shadows are much sharper. But, since the bulb is a disk (albeit small), the shadow has a thin transition zone.]

Op10C POINT-SOURCE LAMP: Plug in a quartz-halogen lamp and turn it on. We are hardly able to look at such a lamp directly. The classroom is full of spectral, sharp shadows, in extreme contrast to the Japanese lantern. One need not repeat the probe with the students as above in Op 10A and Op 10B. Each situation can be investigated from behind an outstretched hand.

CONCLUDING EXPERIMENTS

A variety of final experiments could be done if there is time: Compare sunset to sunrise. Walk through a landscape and notice how the shadows form a coherent whole. Observe the halo around the shadow of your head cast on dewy grass. Observe the clouds at sunrise, mid-morning, noon, etc.

Grade 6 Heat

INTRODUCTION

After Acoustics and Optics comes Heat. Unfortunately, school physics today bases all warmth and cold sensations on a measurable temperature supposedly originating in the amount of heat [energy] in a body, which in turn is imagined as a collection of particles. Whatever pedagogic value such a narrow focusing on the quantitative may have in one or another placement in the curriculum, and the effect model conceptualizing has on the education of thinking, is discussed by me in other places.[1] Here, one should avoid this sort of thing. It is of much more value to see the connections warmth has as it acts in the most varied world phenomena, certainly more manifold than where it appears measurably. We can tie this qualitative experience of warmth into the whole spectrum of nature processes. The clearest perceptions are obtained by completely immersing oneself in the experiences of warmth—of wind, of water, of fire, and so forth.

However, one may not think that simply participating in a warmth condition with our body leads directly to true concepts, or that raw experience will, of itself, lead to understanding. Rather, we first fashion such understanding by reflectively collecting together the widely separated world events which we have experienced in the above way; we must cultivate the experiential. But we have not yet reached the goal. Utilization of only a finger as temperature sensor, for example, leads into the realm of externally measuring warmth with a thermometer, in which something purely mechanical-phoronomical (expansion in one dimension of the mercury in the thermometer) will suppress everything else in the richness of our experience as regards heat. Naturally, we will take up the thermometer in due course, better done in grade 7. While in grade 6, the children ought to understand warmth and cold in more fundamental ways.

I. FROM MOLTEN METAL TO ICE

As introduction to heat and warmth, we begin with the hottest, and proceed slowly along a spectrum to experiencing something ice-cold. Thereby, we can develop a qualitative scale, something like the following series.

THE TERMS "MOLTEN" AND "BOILING HOT" refer to the realm of "dark heat," where an inner light is not yet seen as with "glowing heat." The heated body still retains its own color. To demonstrate this, we show simmering hot molten lead, with its clean, bright and

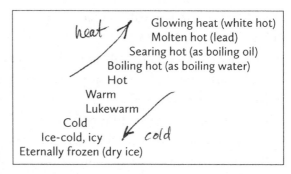

shiny metallic surface color (He1). The bubbling and popping which occurs when water comes in contact with molten lead, or lead with water, shows [qualitatively] that the lead is at a greater heat than water can endure.

What actually is "boiling hot" water? We show this by means of the noise-of-pouring experiment (He3). There is also a well-known viscosity experiment (cohesiveness), where water at various temperatures is passed through a kink in a thin tube (capillary); above is a filling dropper, and we measure the quantity of water flowing through (in drops) and measure the time. Therein, we certainly have obtained an objective measurement, but we have experienced the thing only in an outer way. In contrast, with the experiment (He3) which spreads out water over a surface, we seek to lay open the inner nature of the fluid, so that it may speak directly to the onlooker's sense of movement in images of flowing wave forms. And the difference between soap bubbles made with cold and with hot water is very distinctive: those from hot water are small and short-lived. Also, when we pour in soda water or introduce ink drops, we get very different results with hot and cold water. Both of these lengthy demonstrations can be combined with the heating experiment (He4). Only cold water exhibits the typical wave forms and splashing sounds with pouring. Cold water is actually the first "true" water. We are reminded that, considering the earth as a whole, the cold waters of polar regions are full of life (or were before the onset of humankind). In cold water, life does not die out but engenders swarms of fishes, whales and seals, which multiply there in uncounted multitudes. In contrast, the warm waters of the tropics shelter the most amazing species, however seldom in such numbers.

ICE AND SNOW lead us out of the realm of animate water (including cold water) into the inanimate and crystallized. Its effect on sentient living beings consists, e.g., in a local numbing (He6); upon inanimate things its effect is rigidification, solidification. With the natural fats, one speaks of a "solidification point." At -12°C, or 10.4°F, sunflower oil solidifies, that is, it becomes sirupy and doesn't run out of an inverted container within 10 seconds. In contrast, rapeseed (colza) oil solidifies already at 0°C, 32°F, albeit very slowly; raw cocoa fat around +12°C, or 53.6°F, and tallow even at +32 to 36°C (89.6° to 96.8°F). For fats, solidifying doesn't mean to become a rigid block, but only to form a cohesive, fluffy, viscous material, a grease saturated with oil. With water it is quite different: it freezes into ice, massive and non-porous (with fresh water). The themes of lame, stiff, rigid and solidified can be followed out into many natural realms.

One astonishing fact about ice is its transient melting under pressure, e.g., under the blade of ice skates. Something of this can be demonstrated with an ice block which is cut through by a wire (He7). The strong downward pressure concentrated in the wire permits the water to melt there, clearly without the ice having become warm. The water then *re-freezes* above the wire, which has shifted downward, meanwhile keeping the two halves of the block together. The inclination to rigidity is only overcome in the meltwater obtained below the wire, due to outer heat.

II. SETTING AGLOW [ENKINDLING] AND DYING GLOW [BURNING OUT]

The realm of warmth, with its simmering and bubbling processes within the range of fluid water temperatures, adjoins a realm of cold on one side, where everything becomes rigid, individual bodies, and on the other side the realm of a merging into oneness: the uniform colors of glowing heat, melting together and vaporizing.

GRAY HEAT. If one heats a stone or piece of metal above the melting point of tin (232°C or 450°F), we reach the melting point of lead (327°C or 621°F); lead shavings strewn about now coalesce. Heating further, the pieces begin to give out a weak surface glow, as seen in a pitch-dark room; in this new whitish-gray aspect, the body becomes distinct in color from its surroundings, and one has the impression it is self-bright. (see Optics) This first sensation of brightness, always appearing peripherally to our view, is found at 520–540°C (968-1004°F). At 550°C (1022°F) a reddish glow begins, though visible only in a pitch-dark room; in room light, it appears as brownish.

BRIGHT GLOW, visible even in full daylight, is first met as a brown-red glow at 650°C (1202°F). At 800°C (1472°F) it becomes bright cherry-red, at 1000°C (1832°F) a brilliant yellow-orange, at 1100°C (2012°F) bright yellow, and at 1200°C (2192°F) a radiant white-yellow. These temperature numbers will probably help the teacher's orientation, but for the students, the sensations are the most interesting, e.g., how the colors of gray iron and silver (or even gold) become similar as glowing heat is approached (He8). While cold makes everything in nature hard, solid, and thereby forms separate, individual bodies, in contrast, warmth works to create a unifying, fluidizing, an interchange of one with another, a oneness, which is also expressed in the uniform color of glowing heat attained by all bodies heated to this stage.

III. IMAGES FOR HEAT

On the basis outlined here, in these first heat studies we forgo definitions, measurements and calculations. Instead of delving into "watt-seconds" or material thermodynamics and atoms, we want to expand the whole consideration of the connections manifested in the process of becoming warm or cold. In order to show the kinship of warmth with the most varied world phenomena, one might tie in experiments with the warm and cold colors (He9) next.

From where does earthly coldness come? At a depth of 30cm (12 inches), the earth shows a daily variation[2] of about 2°C (3.6°F), and an annual variation[3] of approximately 17°C (30.6°F), which is very dependent on the soil type.[4] Between 3m and 30m (10 to 100 feet) depth, an average annual temperature range of 8° to 10°C (14–18°F) (+1 degree) happens to prevail in central Europe, depending on time of year and climate. Deeper, the temperature slowly rises with depth, approximately 1°C/100m [0.6°F/100ft) in crystalline granite (to nearly 125°C/100m [75°F/100ft] in Canada); 1°/30m (1.8°F/100ft) in sedimentary rock; and in volcanic areas, 1°/11m (5.4°F/100ft)or so, for example in the Swabian Alps. [These temperature figures are not class material, but an aid to the teacher in developing the basic concepts needed.] It is also warm in mines. The cold cannot come from below upward; it comes from the places on the earth open to the cosmos. This openness to the dark cosmic spaces, with their coldly shimmering stars, is the actual phenomenon; heat radiation (re-radiation) is a superfluous, adjunct concept.

From where does warmth come? All changes in terrestrial warmth of the earth's surface arise from the orientation toward the sun and its rhythms. Open earthly surfaces, that is, freely exposed to the sun, get warm. The dark expanse of the starry heavens with their constellations eternally fixed together (which actually circle about us, geocentrically) is a static image of cold. In contrast, the sun moves everything on earth and guides the course of the day and the year with its journey, allowing us to have feelings [as an internal ebb and flow in soul]. The sun becomes for us the never-resting image of warmth. We recall the poem of Morgenstern: "Oh See the Land of Dawn." Cold and warmth relate to mental imagination and willing, if one understands these in the sense of Rudolf Steiner's anthropology (*Study of Man* lectures).

In the kingdom of nature, the animal phyla increase their body temperature up to the stage of being warm-blooded (internally maintaining an elevated body temperature). Amphibians and reptiles (invertebrates) utilize outer warmth. Then the birds and finally the mammals maintain an inner warmth against outer variations. And warmth in the human being is different again. This warmth not only comes from the interaction between nature and the soul activity adjacent to the body (as with the higher animals) but arises from the spirit, insofar as the human being works out of goals conceived in spirit. Then he gets "warm" for the matter at hand. And, with the will, he takes hold of the streaming warmth of the entire body and also the adjacent air, often making it warmer around him.

Through the activity of the cosmos, the warmth of the sun develops ever anew out of coldness (starry night). Nature pulsates with this warmth. In human deeds, intentions develop out of conceptual coldness, and, through a love for doing, new warmth is engendered in the world [in addition to the warmth directly attributable to the sun]. In warmth, cosmic and human processes come into contact. The outer warmth of the sun seems like the will of a spread-out being; and the warmth developed in the human being seems like an individualized warmth of the cosmos. Thinking through such relationships of warmth leads to a view of the world which encompasses the human being. Rudolf Steiner has taken this up in the "Warmth Course,"[5] in contrast to the "Light Course,"[6] where a scientific method appropriate to light is sketched out. (see Optics, above)

IV. THERMAL INSULATION

In order to show the kinship of warmth with the most varied phenomena of the world, we might tie in an experiment about warm and cold colors and sounds (He9), perhaps placing it as an introduction to the heat studies.

We have not given a technical treatment to the subject of warmth; that starts in 7th grade and increases in 8th and 9th grades, leading up to heat engines (steam and internal combustion). We have considered warmth less from the point of view of technical goals of people, but rather from the viewpoint of a wellspring of cosmic force. That leads us to the human will. To the extent this is inserted into the world in a humanized, cultivated way, a new and distinctive problem arises, that of warm clothing. The will of the human being does not always manifest itself nakedly in the world with raw power, but via clothing, the attempt is made to hold back our warmth in order to direct it with our will, and also to allow it to be active within our own soul.

Thus, warmth, in the image of clothing, leads us to the theme: externalized will, internalized will. Each human being can produce a kind of warmth island, an *insula*. For this thermal insulators are needed: things which permit warmth to be maintained in close proximity to cold. As this is realized, these questions lead us to practical questions of clothing fabrics and weaving, so that a bit of study of topics from daily life (*Lebenskunde*) may enter into our studies in a conventional sense. And the concept of thermal insulators (dry, light, airy, not watery) is a preparation for the concept of electrical insulators.

Experiments in Heat

HE 1 MELTING; "MOLTEN HOT"

Place a bar of tin solder (still available in some plumbers' supply shops) or simple commercial tin ingot, about a half cup, in a small pot [a old plumber's "solder pot" of cast iron is excellent] and heat it up on a lab tripod over a Fisher burner. Heat it until approximately half a minute past the molten point. Then, dribble cold water onto the surface of the molten metal until it no longer vaporizes and sizzles: our "broth" greatly exceeds the boiling temperature of water. We show how the tin has become rigid through this by inverting the pot; a solid lump falls out.

Then, we re-heat it (for 10 to 20 seconds beyond melting) and then let the molten metal run down a trough with wood sides into a large bucket of water in a glittering stream. Note: If we heat it too long, it will be too hot and will sputter too violently in the water (safety glasses are necessary). But if heated to just past the melting point, it will solidify on the board. The plywood track, about 50 cm (20") long, may be set up at a slope of less than 45°. [Note how it sears the wood; it is even hotter than the scorching temperature for wood. Observe the fascinating frozen splash-forms found at the bottom of the bucket.]

HE 2 NOISE OF POURING

Prepare two 2-liter (2-quart) saucepans, one filled with cold water and another with boiling water. Alternately pour liquid from each, cup by cup, into two porcelain basins, which should be as large and strong as possible. Listen to the smacking and splashing of the cold water and the puffing of the hot water, which pours like velvet. One could also listen to water poured into a baby-bath with hand towels spread out inside and placed on a concrete floor.

HE 3 FLOWING FORMS

Set up a plywood runway, approximately 130cm x 80cm x 1cm (50" x 30" x 3/8") as follows: The board has twice been rubbed with linseed oil and 2 hours later buffed with a cloth to remove excess oil. The pores of the wood are thereby sealed. It is illuminated from below with our lab lamp (100 watt, with collimating reflector; alternatively, use a quartz-halogen auto headlamp). Adjust the lamp so it shines on the wave fronts and makes them glisten. First we pour hot water over it in order to moisten the board. Then we alternate between ice-cold water (don't pour out the required ice cubes) and hot water (only at about 70°C [94°F], so it doesn't produce steam to confuse things). If the board has achieved the same temperature through repeated pourings, different wave forms and also different flow times are observed. Is is astonishing how abundant and undulating the runoff is for cold water.

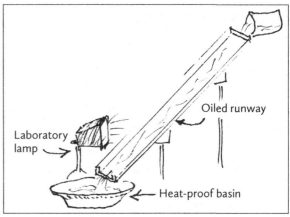

Revealing water in flowing forms

HE 4 DROPS AND BUBBLES

COMPARISON: In the simplest form, one places a beaker of cold tap water next to a similar one with the same amount of already boiling water; then, we introduce ink drops. In the boiling water, the ink drops sink differently, and the boiling bubbles make a "stormy" scene. [In cooler water, interesting garland ring-forms arise, and persist longer; while the warm water dissolves forms so quickly that the ink drops very rapidly become diffused, and interesting shapes do not last long enough to appreciate them.]

HEATING: Fix a 600 ml beaker of pyrex (with low thermal expansion coefficient) with a clamp over a tripod stand, and fill it with soda water and ice cubes so that we can see the surface under the clamp. We heat it with a lab burner, which is turned to a blue flame but not too large. If the flame is too sharp or not fanned back and forth, the glass will fracture. But if we heat it too weakly, the demonstration will take too long and not be very interesting.

When the ice has finally just melted, sample the warmth: No greater heat is detectable, despite the time over heat (the ice has kept it cool). Allow the water to become still, and observe ink drops. They sink slowly and with interesting forms, visually showing the water is cool. When we heat the water again, the ink color disappears via heat [especially true with washable ink] and through dispersion. We continue to introduce ink drops, although with stronger heating, we can drop in ink for only a short while, since the bubbles (carbon dioxide) rise in more wavy paths. The ink sinks more rapidly now. Finally, we hear the sound of boiling, and the water is in chaos as shown by ink dropped in again.

HE 5 NUMBING BY COLD

Smash an ice block from the ice tray (or frozen in a bread pan) between two towels. Note the sound of crushing. [It will sound brittle, glassy, especially if the ice is really cold.] A hand rubbed between the sharp fragments would be cut. Now every child receives a walnut-size fragment, and rubs it on a soft place, perhaps the inside of the arm, for as long as she can stand it. Just poke at the skin with a needle or a sharp pin. She can't distinguish the first skin contact, as before; instead, she will feel only a strange pressure sensation.

HE 6 STIFFENING

Have a student plunge his hand into a beaker full of ice water. When it becomes uncomfortable, have him take his hand out, showing the reddened skin. His attempts to tie a ribbon or play a violin show the fingers can move only slowly and clumsily; he has lost dexterity. This experiment is only an example, since the fingers knot up when the whole body is too severely attacked. [Cold like this is actually a physiological trauma to the body, and should not be carried too far; also, we could relate the stories of people's experiences in falling through the ice in accidents, etc.]

HE 7 ICE BLOCK

Place an ice block, frozen in a bread pan, on two blocks or stools. Drape piano wire over the block, having earlier investigated the maximum weight at which the wire won't break. Also, we must let the freezing cold ice block sit out for a while, allowing the surface and the interior to equalize to 0°C (32°F).

Over a period of 1 to 2 hours, the wire will pass down through the ice block and the block will remain unbroken. Only at the end will the wire split out a fragment as the weights fall to the floor (covered with mats). The larger the weights relative to the wire, the more quickly it will pass through. With very thin wire (e.g., thinnest piano wire), the experiment goes amazingly fast. However, if the ice is colder than -2°C (28.4°F), the wire will not pass through.

The uncut ice block mystery

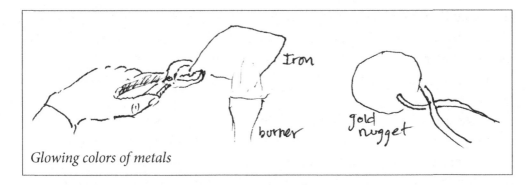

Glowing colors of metals

HE 8 GLOWING METALS

Heat both a rusty piece of iron plate about 5mm (3/16") thick, cut into a diamond shape, and a small nugget of gold to glowing. [Real, pure gold will be unharmed! but don't heat it beyond an orange glow or it could melt.] Hold the pieces over the blue cone of the flame in a semi-dark room, and heat just to a visible glow. In a totally breathtaking way, the gold takes on a peach blossom hue, in contrast to the very red color of the iron.

HE 9 COLD AND WARM COLORS AND SOUNDS

Set up five 250ml Erlenmeyer flasks with colored solutions. One is filled with a saturated iron (III) chloride salt solution [brownish-red]; alternatively, iron (III) nitrate can be used. A second contains a saturated solution of copper (II) sulfate [sky blue]; the third, with the same copper salt solution, but with potassium chloride solution added (until it is turquoise but not too dark). The fourth has potassium and sodium chloride (table salt) solutions with hydrochloric acid added,

and a sufficient amount of copper (II) sulfate to make a strong green. The fifth flask contains a potassium dichromate solution [deep orange]. Also, place a flat-bottomed Florence flask on the lecture table, supported by rubber stoppers so that it can be illuminated by our lab lamp, and the colors projected onto the classroom wall.

The expansiveness and stillness of the blue and the almost tangible coldness of the turquoise contrast to the proximity and warmth of the orange-red of the iron salts. These transparent mineral colors resemble the transparently colored precious stones.

For the "cold" and "warm" sounds, we use similarly sized wood and metal rods or plates. [Recall our explorations at the end of Acoustics.]

Grade 6 Electricity

INTRODUCTION

In studying electricity, we should strive not for a system of classification, but for a complete unfolding of the impressions for this peculiar realm, to open the path to experiences in a new realm of feelings, which should be treated imagistically. This should be unified with a few clear concepts. This realm unlocks itself only slightly for teachers not schooled in phenomenology—also in considering the experiments—so much so that they scarcely know how to characterize or present it. Therefore, along with the teaching indications, we must generally ponder many things about electricity in addition, not in order to make this subject clear, but to keep its truly enigmatic character clearly in view so that, through teaching directed at a clear goal, the students can be brought to a clear experience of it.

I. THE HISTORY OF ELECTRICITY

THE HISTORY of a subject is already the thing itself—almost. How was electricity discovered? How was it first made? Since antiquity, amber was circulated widely.[1] It was traded from the Baltic sea to Greece, and was also mined in Silesia and the Po delta. The Greeks called it *elektron*, meaning "clear yellow." After Thales—who described it—people knew that once rubbed vigorously with fur, an attractive influence arose, such that cotton or wool fibers, papyrus scraps and animal hairs were attracted to it.

The Greeks thought of amber as coagulated tears, so it was entwined with the myths of those who died tragically and were bewailed with "amber tears." Though the Romans were already clear about the obvious nature of amber (hardened resin), this electric force of amber remained un-researched for 2000 years—while acoustics, optics and above all mechanics were constantly elaborated and advanced step by step.

IN ENGLAND, electricity was investigated further only at the end of the 16th century. What was breaking through at this time? The rulership of the entire island kingdom had finally transferred from the clan chieftains of the Scottish highlands and from the Scottish royal houses to the English crown, which reigned from London, the great city with a seaport. Mary Stuart fell, and Elizabeth I led the island to the beginning of its greatest power. She cut herself off from the old powers; the Anglican church was established and the Roman church in England decisively suppressed. Shakespeare's dramas appeal to a person's individual power over his or her fate. The Pope hurled a papal bull over the water; the Armada followed. Elizabeth held steady, cultivated rulership of the seas and founded a worldly kingdom. Her physician, William Gilbert (1544–1603), was truly the most outstanding natural scientist of his time. His life work was on magnetism, on which he did basic research, and he proposed it as a useful means of orientation at sea, independent of mechanical artifice and no longer based on [the sailor's lore of] water currents, clouds or sky. Gilbert delineated the electrical forces on the one hand, and meanwhile also presented their phenomena in essential ways. With his fluid hypothesis, he presented the first comprehensive theory of electricity. The word *electricity* is derived from Gilbert's *vis electrica*: Electricity (from *electricus* meaing "of amber") was then called "a force of amber."

Since then electricity was developed via Franklin, who put Gilbert's ideas into practice and advanced them; via Galvani to Volta, who utilized Galvani's ideas and advanced them; then via Faraday, who developed Siemens' ideas. Following these three steps also—Gilbert-Franklin, Galvani-Volta, Faraday-Siemens—our curriculum develops for the 6th, 7th and 8th grades. It begins in London with Gilbert, who was the first to probe and cultivate man-made electrical phenomena which pierce the cohesive tapestry of nature, and to study them with a zeal previously devoted to observing naturally occurring objects of creation. One can relate the biography of Elizabeth I and can recognize in it the voice of this age, as it was experienced in the somewhat misguided form of this great surrender to the external world; in it, there are many things we can bring up to the students as related topics throughout this block.

II. HOW IT ARISES AND SUBSIDES

HOW IT ARISES AND SUBSIDES is a useful way of externally classifying the most enigmatic things in the world. Attraction is the first noticeable phenomenon which shows that an object has some special property or state. Representative of the sort of awareness that prevailed for 2000 years, we begin with two natural objects: amber and a piece of fur (El1).

With the attraction of paper scraps we see the qualities that are especially suited for generating an electrified state: light, dry, thin, and usually flammable materials—also articles that are dried out and dead (El2). These are at the same time materials which are resistant to warmth and cold, so-called thermal insulators. These dead things must be pressed together in intimate contact and then separated. After rubbing or pressing, they are inclined to stick to each other: It is this separation against the resistance (especially noticeable with plastic materials) which creates the electrical tension [static electric charge].[2] Thus, an equally strong counter-pole arises simultaneously in the rubbing material (table surface); however, it usually passes into the earth through physical contact and vanishes as soon as it is created. The pulling-together which attraction seeks to bring about is a kind of answer to the foregoing ritual of separation—both mechanical gestures [the separation and the subsequent attraction] are dependent on each other, albeit usually misunderstood. However, this rubbed or stroked material even attracts other materials, even lightweight metal bodies if they are suspended on a string [and thus prevented from grounding away the polar electric charge induced in them].

It is useful to obtain the phenomena more powerfully by using plastic articles. Now, repulsive forces really make their appearance (El3). As we see plainly, once the scraps have taken up the condition of the foil itself, they are repelled. Attraction, in contrast, becomes what the condition does not have. The wad flies out into the room; it jumps away in aversion. The fact that the objects fall to the side, not downward, is significant. Despite their individualization, the parts of our earth instead form a great whole; this is manifest in falling, where everything moves toward a union with the earth. Everything which has been raised up above the earth's surface or up into the air shows that it belongs to the underlying mass of the earth by the weight with which it presses down on other things.

This unity, which encompasses all material objects and is apparent in their weight and falling motion, is shattered by electrical force: The wad "falls" to the side, onto the film, rather than downward as usual. In place of the all-encompassing connection with the earth, we see the creation of an individual-seeking center, which falls out of the interwoven web of world phenomena. Plastic materials have, of themselves, an inclination to this state, allowing it to be created very strongly in them, so that one can hardly even get rid of it. As a rule, all the attracted bodies contribute to its elimination: the air to a lesser degree, and even less everything which has a connection with the earth. By means of the earth, and also the human hand, we can clear away the ghost of the electrification—usually. But through the necessary touch and the subsequent separation, a new electrification will often be produced. The "healing power" of the whole earth can eliminate these most stubborn charges via water, the wet bowl, the table, the floor, to the earth (El4). The earth swallows up these observable charges and normalizes the situation. We have already found this out: One can generate an electrification only in dry conditions, and also only with dead things which are no longer permeated with a water-filled life. The electric state cannot be produced with leather and wood, which are porous and which very delicately exchange moisture with the air. Also a flame in the neighborhood eliminates the electrified state very quickly. Electricity resides outside of the play of elements, resides entirely in the solid or even in some other realm.

Unseen, the image creeps in that electricity is an "illness" which is "healed" by water and by Mother Earth. We allow this comparison to be held provisionally, since it expresses something of our experience (not for any other essential reason). Later, we will give it up [in the more "conventional" electric studies of grade 7, etc.].

III. CONDUCTORS AND INSULATORS

CONDUCTION AND INSULATION as basic concepts of electricity should now be worked out. At first insulation from the electrical state is incomprehensible in certain materials (El 5). After rubbing, the charge sits solidly there, anyway. When we run into such an "electrical nest," such a crackling and charged place, then it can be removed with a small thrust of the finger, without the neighboring "nest" disappearing! Also, the electrically charged condition is not present to the same degree everywhere on the rod (mostly owing to unequal rubbing, irregularities in the surface…). It has a localized activity, and these localities do not act together; they are separated from one another like islands. The rod isolates the condition, it "insulates;" (*insula*, Latin = island). The thermal insulators utilized to generate frictional electricity also show themselves to be electrical insulators. In contrast to these, there are materials which unite themselves wholly with the electrified state, spreading it as much as possible. These are called "conductors."

We can compare the electrified state to some sort of invisible material something, which can be collected in droplets: the larger the container, the more "fits inside." As further experiments show, for example inverting the jar, it doesn't depend on the inner volume nor on the surface available inside, rather the static electric capacity depends only on the exterior surface. Strangely, it is immaterial onto which side of the object one strokes the electricity, and where one eliminates it. The metal object is always "loaded" as a whole and discharged as a whole. Clearly, it merges together every electric charge stroked onto it, accumulates it, and even spreads it out to the tips of the paper strips. Their spreading out shows the gradual increase of electrical charge. And then, in a blast, everything "available" discharges from some arbitrary spot. Thus, the metal can is a conductor, distributing the charge all over its surface.

The laborious charging of a metal object using a rubbed rod can also be accomplished by machine: the Guericke Electric Machine (El7).[3] It was discovered by the mayor of Magdeburg, Baron von Guericke, and is still fascinating today. Guericke connected to it all sorts of ideas about earth forces.

A kind of tension [as in high-tension electricity] even takes hold of the experimenter: A person becomes nervous because she never sees beforehand how powerful a spark will arise. The interconnection of perceptions, and even time and space are somehow overcome. Everything else in our world develops: Plants grow and clouds sail across the sky. Here, however, something occurs instantly and unheralded, after a kind of enigmatic, almost ritual preparation.

IV. WHAT IS ELECTRICITY?

This question can hardly be answered by conjecture or out of books. Only a thoughtful, personal experience of the perceptions will help us along, though at first only to the point where we can ask questions. The significant thing is that as we get to know the perceptions from the most varied sense realms and see how they occur unexpectedly, we sense that the manifestations of electricity have no connection with ordinary nature, and actually we perceive little of electricity itself. From where comes the prick in my finger even though there is nothing closer than 3mm or 1/8 inch? The phenomena which manifest at first do truly indicate some condition, though not its essential form; rather, they only point to its disappearance. Thus, the spark (so typical of electricity) discharges in a burst. The attracted paper scraps decrease the tension only a little, though they screen it off toward the outside. The repelled [scraps] diminish the electric charge and carry some of it off to be neutralized. And the erect paper strips grope about in the surroundings seeking to set loose the charge. Attraction, repulsion, crackling and sparks: All are already on the way to the disappearance of the electrified state; they arise in answer to the "engendering" ritual.

But what is actually engendered? Phenomena of disappearance! The state itself—if such a thing exists—veils itself, lying beneath the tapestry of perceptions. Nevertheless, something works out from under it: Things are set in motion as if by a spirit hand. From distant places sparks and heat are manifest. A sort of illusory life arises. Animate objects, green plants, wood and leather must forsake giving rise to it; we must use brittle, dried up, dead things, press them together and then separate them: Thereupon occurs some sort of unanticipated illusory life. Thereby we move out of the realm of the dead (which leads to stillness, heaviness and rigidity), out into an unforeseen territory—but from a different side, not back toward life.

Electricity is alien to living nature. We pierce through into a sub-dead place, the so-called realm of "sub-nature" (Steiner), where rigidity dissolves and a new "life" of activity sets in. With sub-nature I don't mean to suggest a mythical region, but I am attempting to comprehend and characterize that which we experience, that is, to think about the connection with the experienceable world.

V. IMAGES FOR ELECTRICITY

For teaching, we must seek to comprehend such ideas in images, since, just when we have really impressive, exciting experiments to bring to the class, the students are inclined to experience only the side of the power of the effects. The life of feeling takes on an egoistic orientation, an experience of controlling the world[4] and phenomena become a means for entertainment. The feeling life is shut off from the world, becomes a stereotype, and finally narrows down to only their own physical bodies. The pedagogical task of this second seven-year period is the opposite: differentiation of the feelings by a full illumination of the human, not a mere utilitarian and representational meeting with the world. It is valuable to build up conceptualizations which work in a sense-illumined manner, which are not abstract but can be felt as objective images. A comprehensive basis for the comparative, imagistic approach is given by Steiner in his education lectures. Here we have to ask the question: What sort of image exactly?

The picture elaborated above of illness and healing is only partly valid. Electricity is fundamentally so alien to nature that one cannot actually speak of illness or hostility. Only on the boundaries, when it works excessively out from what is dead does it make life ill. In general, electricity doesn't eliminate life, but it shoves itself in between without connection. Historically the familiarity with it began— as outlined above—with the onset of the consciousness-soul age and the desire to penetrate inanimate nature. Electricity—even for the electrical hobbyist—should not be be allowed to be applied to this goal. A possibility might be an image like the following: one wanders through a completely dead, rolling landscape toward an unimaginably vast, black sea in a rocky depression. It shimmers like water, iridescent in its almost metallic blackness. And, when we attempt to poke into it with a stick, the stick is thrown back, and we ourselves get a shock. Constantly new, unexpected reactions happen, and we cannot manage to grasp any of this "sea" in our hands or to successfully penetrate into it.

Prosaic school physics also goes in for pictures: the so-called model. Although electrical phenomena do not occur directly on the bodies but in their environment (jumping sparks, attraction ...), one thinks of all this as caused by a quasi-material "load or charge," which sits "on" the body and is collected or spread out and always remains preserved. Thus the school physics must suppose that since these charges arise out of nothingness (the rubbing) and disappear into the void with neutralization of plus and minus (which we do not yet introduce), or through grounding, plus and minus charges must therefore be available in equal amounts in all matter. Since they are neutralized (swallowed up) in all experiments, they must be distributed in atomically separate particles, which are in everything. It is as if the world is made of electricity.

This brief peek into conventional theories may suffice. This material-electrical model does not have to be precisely portrayed (it is found in public school textbooks) nor must its epistemological justification be evaluated—that is, it should be left completely open. Here, we are only evaluating its pictorial character for introductory lessons. To what extent can it be not only an intellectual model, but a symbol for the phenomena? As symbol, it sets the phenomena topsy turvy. Electricity is sub-nature, or at least beside the whole of nature insofar as we characterize in plain phenomena. By means of such models, electricity is turned into an all-permeating foundation; the world is inwardly electrified and atomized. The inner, essential aspect of the world will thereby be made inaccessible to human participation, shoved into atomic tininess, i.e., abducted.

The child will be shut out of the free world. So, this picture works destructively on the soul. Natural science teaching may not responsibly get entangled in the scientifically oriented phenomenal character of contradicting theories, but rather it demands of the teacher a consideration of the fundamental perceptions. And, if science and our culture do without this consideration, then the teacher can implant it into culture by his example. In any case, he must also have planted it in himself.

VI. FURTHER ELECTRICITY EXPERIMENTS

Further electrical phenomena can be shown in abundance; the needle effect [discharge from needle points, causing a wheel to turn], the generation of "vitreous" [plus] and "resinous" [minus] kinds of charge (the latter with glass and silk), the spreading out of dry tissue scraps, etc. All these demonstrations can hardly take place in the time available. Even the reverse is prone to happen, even if we have enough time. The point is not so much to complete a chapter in physics, but rather to dive deep down into the way to experience this subject, thereby dredging up illuminated pictures. A packed syllabus and a materialistic approach proffers stones instead of bread to the student's awakening interest in the world. But if, instead of pursuing a subject systematically, one takes a swing into an entirely different field of experience, then one fosters interest. Then, along with unfolding these new and characteristic phenomena, totally different and unfamiliar feelings will begin afresh each day. Such new feelings will be developed and differentiated step by step, through further considerations and comparisons, as the students grow older.

Experiments in Elecricity

EL 1 AMBER

Introduce as large as possible a piece of amber or violin rosin; tell the students about the Greek name *elektron* (ελεκτρον) and the Germanic name for amber, *burnable stone*. Then, rub it a few times with a piece of fur (which has been washed like clothing in the washing machine to remove the natural oil, if necessary). Cut up pieces of paper (wrapping tissue or tracing paper) in front of the students and place them on a dark carton or book cover; they will be attracted to and stick to the "charged" or "electrified" amber. [Test other objects as well; dry, dead things work best.]

EL 2 HEATED ELECTRICAL CHARGES

Lay a piece of regular copy paper on the varnished or plastic surface of a clean table (thoroughly cleaned). Stroke it rapidly with both hands, from the center outward, all over the paper. Peel the sheet up, and hold it over the paper scraps (from El1): no reaction. However, if the paper and also the table surface are warmed with a hair dryer, then it usually happens that a few of the smaller scraps are attracted. [Note that it is the intimate contact, not the rubbing, that is the essential part of the treatment. Once separated, nature tends to resist this by attracting the things back together.]

EL 3 JUMPING WAD

Lay out a plastic film on a dry surface (wood, formica, or other synthetic), possibly heated with a blow dryer. Stroke over the entire surface with the edges of the hand. When pulled away, the film sticks onto the surface. Its underside is utilized in the experiments:

We initially show how paper scraps usually jump onto it. After a few seconds, however, many of them splay out, jump off, and are repelled from it.

Show how the film is attracted to a marble-sized paper wad suspended a few centimeters away. Pulling the film away, the wad which was stuck onto it now jumps away; this time, a greater distance away. If we drop a fresh wad to fall from a distance of about 1–2 hands away in front of the film, it doesn't fall straight down; its path curves to the side—it is diverted and jumps toward the film.

EL 4 HEALING UP: SOOTHING ELECTRICAL TENSION

For a conclusion, we attempt to make the film or rod unelectrified by stroking it on both sides with open hands. Nevertheless, it always attracts scraps in several places. Then hold it with clamps on a lab stand and bathe it briefly in water; dry it with a hair dryer held about 1m (a yard) away. The film or rod is "normalized" or grounded; the charge has disappeared—no scraps are attracted!

[Note the ritual procedure necessary to produce the effects; then, we observe strange jumping or movement.]

EL 5 INSULATING; ISLANDS OF CHARGE

Introduce a rod (about 40cm or 16" long) of glass, hard rubber, or, even better, PVC pipe. Rub it with light pressure with wool. Drawing the wool away, we will hear crackling.

- Move a finger alongside the rod, about 1cm (½") away. From many places, unexpected sparks crackle, which in room light are not usually seen, but can be felt as small pricks in the skin.
- Pass a fluorescent lamp near the rubbed rod instead of the fingers, or rubbed instead of the rod: numerous irregular sparkling lights.
- Wiping electricity off with our hand removes the capacity for pricks in Step 1, but not entirely the sparking of the fluorescent tube in Step 2.

EL 6A CONDUCTORS

Place a large metal object *which has no sharp points or corners* (e.g., an old-fashioned metal marmalade jar) on top of various materials, starting with a plastic [pencil-]

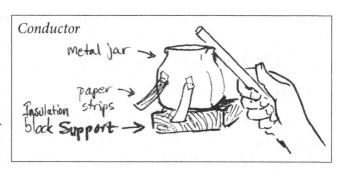

box. On the lower part of the jar, at two locations visible to the audience, we tape two finger-length strips of onion-skin paper or tissue. Stroke a rod electrified by rubbing (El5) repeatedly against this metal object; the paper strips spread out. Then with a finger, we approach that place where we have stroked the charge onto the object: at a 1mm (1/16")distance, a spark jumps out which is brighter, louder and more painful than those achieved with the rod alone (in El5). Repeatedly bringing a finger close causes nothing much further. Electrification and subsequent discharging at other spots causes much the same results.

EL 6B INSULATORS

We can vary the insulation blocks (wood, glass, leather, porcelain, etc.). For example, the paper strips sink down faster with wood, or even do not stand out at all. We can also vary the size of the metal object: Larger sizes correspond with stronger sparks. If we fill the jar with water, sparks can even be obtained from the surface of the water, even using a piece of ice! Instead of a metal object, have a student, standing on an insulating pedestal (e.g., with plastic legs made of short, thick lucite rods), gradually be charged up. When he makes contact with another student, the spark is very strong. [Thus insulators allow the charge to be accumulated and to persist, while conductors constantly annihilate any charge and prevent it from accumulating.]

EL 7A ELECTRIC MACHINE

Basically, the von Guericke electrification machine is a horizontally mounted cylinder of plastic (e.g., a 3-inch PVC pipe), with a crank affixed to the axle and a rubbing pad and metal comb mounted on the back side to collect the charge.

Using the von Guericke machine, we no longer rub the plastic cylinder with our hand, but with a wool or plastic foam pad. As the drum surface rotates away and separates from the foam, it becomes electrified. On the other side, the rotating drum has a metal comb fixed in close proximity, which becomes electrified even though it doesn't touch the drum; in the dark, we can see a glow in the air near the comb and a large area on the cylinder. The comb is connected to a metal storage

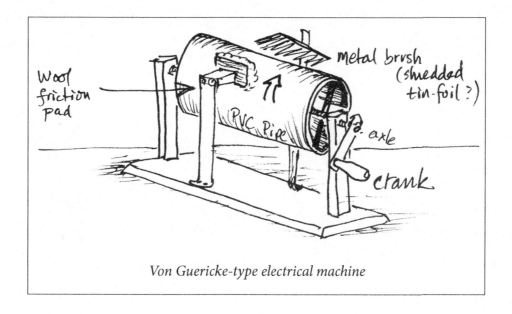

Von Guericke-type electrical machine

plate; sparks up to 3cm (1¼") long can be drawn from this conductor. The brush material (rubber foam) is connected with the metal support bracket and the weakly conductive wood base, the table and the earth, and thus grounded (the same as with manual rubbing, when the material is held in the hand).

[Note: The von Guericke machine is similar to the van de Graaff type—recognizable by its two vertically arranged charge-accumulator spheres, one on top and the other at the base. However, that type has most of the parts enclosed inside, and is therefore more mysterious in its operation, and not as desirable as the older but more understandable von Guericke type. The Wimshurst type, another antique, is crank-driven, with wiring to carry the charges from the brushes to the Leyden jars to accumulate the charge. Although the Wimshurst form is more difficult to make and more expensive because it uses glass discs, rotated in opposite directions, it is capable of generating more current, and is, therefore, more suitable for the glowing tubes investigated in grade 11 physics.]

EL 7B FURTHER ELECTRICAL EXPERIMENTS

If time permits, you could do further experiments with "resinous" and "vitreous" [positive] charges.

Grade 6 Magnetism

INTRODUCTION

Magnetism is placed last in the series of topics for the grade 6 physics block. Usually, only a few days remain in the time available. We cannot undertake too much with magnetism; but we can attempt to create an impression. This can be found in my experiments relating to the natural magnetism of the earth. The compass stands before the children, and the riddle of iron and the iron minerals which show their orientation to north anywhere on earth, so they stand functionally between the directionless, unrelated materials of the solid earth and the spread-out oneness of the celestial dome. The compass is also pertinent to the studies of geography and the Age of Explorers in the history curriculum of grade 6.

I. NATURAL MAGNETISM

Natural magnetism was the only source of this force for centuries, until the discovery of the electric coil magnet by Oersted in 1820. (see experiments about electromagnets: Mag1 and Mag2 in 8th grade) First, we lay a piece of the black iron mineral, magnetite (lodestone), onto a little wooden boat and place it in a large dish of water. Slowly, it turns toward an orientation to which it will return again if disturbed and then left alone (Mag1). During this slow rotation, the following experiment can be presented.

II. MAGNETIZATION

We can create magnetism by stroking a steel compass needle or piece of iron with a fragment of the lodestone, or as follows: Take a steel needle and vibrationally magnetize it by pounding it along its length while holding it oriented pointing diagonally down and to the north. Afterward, hang it up: Now like the floating lodestone, it too will orient itself to the north (Mag2). What does this mean? A piece of ore, when it is made weightless, i.e., placed in a frictionless, mobile support (suspended), will return to the orientation which it had in the mountain, in the vein of ore in which it once lay. The portion of the piece which, as seen from its center, was originally toward the north, will later on move once again toward the north. This fragment of the earth is never disconnected, but retains its connection to its source—not with the particular place from which it came, but to the whole earth, to the northward direction there (also the southward direction). Like a memory, it retains the directionality of its place of origin in the form of a weak force in the fragment. It is the same with the pounded steel needle. It will seek to return again to the position it had during the pounding or vibrating. What the mineral had taken up and preserved over an immeasurably long time, the steel needle has received in minutes.

If pieces of iron remain fixed in position for years, they will also be magnetized by the earth; the longer they remain in an appropriate orientation, the stronger the magnetization. This position is not horizontally northward (as can be investigated by varying Mag2) but northward and downward by about 70°. The actual magnetic direction is only 20° short of the vertical! Thus, for heating ducts, architectural iron rods, and in short, all free-standing iron masses, being maintained in a definite vertical position is sufficient to allow them to be noticeably magnetized over time. The upper parts receive south-seeking (blue type) magnetism and the bottom receives north-seeking (red type) magnetism. Otherwise, a compass needle would point upward with its north-seeking (red) end and downward with its south-seeking (blue) end. The thermal expansion and vibration of the building as a result of occupation over the years has been replaced in Mag2 by the hammering.

The verification of the compass in the form of a magnet acting upon a magnet is better shown in grade 7. If we want to relate how wrought iron becomes magnetized, then we could say: If we take a bar and suspend it so it is free to move, it will assume a north-south alignment. The magnetization by hammering is for the teacher the field within which she can work out the experience of the earth's magnetism, by force, skill and patience.

III. DE-MAGNETIZATION

Next, explore the elimination of magnetism. Iron is just the one among the metals which by its rigidity and hardness equips the forces of the human being to subdue the outer world. Through iron, force is collected and drawn off. How is magnetic force connected to this? Heat a small iron bar, which has perhaps been strongly magnetized by a modern permanent magnet, to glowing and perhaps also hammer it while hot. During the softening induced by heat, the magnetism dwindles, and afterward the bar is de-magnetized (Mag3). The precise temperature of this de-magnetization is termed the "Curie temperature," and for iron is about 780°C (1436°F).

IV. COMPASSES

As the first application of magnetism, the compass is for the students something serious, immense, pointing out into the world (Mag4). The word *compass* stems from the medieval Italian *compassire,* meaning "to happen together" or "to walk about," which the needle does over the compass rose. It should be mentioned that even the best compasses do not point to the true (geographic) north. Also, our hammered needle becomes a tiny bit more magnetic if oriented slightly to the west (for locations east of the Great Lakes; west of this, orient to the east) during the hammering.

We call this deviation of a magnet from true north "declination" or "compass deviation." For eastern North America, it is about 10° west of north, and decreases going west, as Columbus discovered. If we travel by ship northward to locations east of Greenland, to Ireland, Scotland and the Arctic Sea, the westerly deviation increases until the needle points almost west! Then, it doesn't adjust itself any more: the north magnetic pole.

In the area near Alaska, it is all reversed: The deviation is greater to the east. If we travel to Siberia, the needle points almost northeast. As the explorer Ross sought out the location of the north magnetic pole for the first time, it lay beneath the Boothia Felix Peninsula at 70°15'N latitude, 96°45'W longitude. Today it has shifted about to the west, to about 76°N latitude and 100°W longitude, or about 350 km (217 miles). It lies north of Prince of Wales Island in the region of northern Canada, and drifts northeast at about 2 miles/year. The compass needles of the northern hemisphere point approximately to this place. In the southern hemisphere, somewhat simply stated, compasses point to the south magnetic pole at 65°S latitude and 139°E longitude, between Australia and Antarctica in the sea off the Antarctic coast. Forty years ago it lay at 72° latitude and 155° longitude, on the coast of Antarctica. It shifts northward 4 miles/year.

V. MAGNETIC DECLINATION

The following maps indicate the declination over the earth during the last century. Later on, the null line (of 0° deviation) lies further west, as the map below shows. At any given locality, the declination changes, often by as much as 1°/decade, sometimes more. For example, Paris (which was spared during the Thirty Years' War) preserved records of the following measurements.

In Europe, the line of zero declination has shifted from Königsburg (in present East Prussia) to Berlin, also at about 12 miles/year. In addition to this variation over

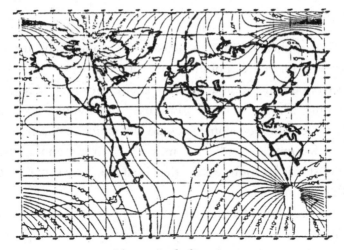

Magnetic declination

Variations in Deviation Over Time		
Date	Declination	
1580	11°	East Dev.
1618	8°	
1663	0°	
1763	8°	West Dev.
1780	17°	
1810	22°	
1852	20°	
1902	15°	
1944	11°	

Recordings in Paris

long intervals, the so-called "secular variation," there is a daily variation, mostly in the strength of the geomagnetic field. This is usually about 0.001 of the overall strength, and is directed toward the sun, and less to the moon; thus the magnetic direction vector is at its weakest at local noon. [The sun vertically overhead deflects the usual northward pull, thus reducing its magnitude.]

VI. MAGNETIC INCLINATION

By "inclination" we mean a deflection downward in addition to the deflection from north (Mag5). At the geographic poles, the inclination is 90° to the horizontal; therefore the field doesn't affect a compass pivoted only horizontally. However, if a compass needle is fixed precisely in the middle with a delicate horizontal axle, it will point to the magnetic pole: downward. In the equatorial regions the inclination

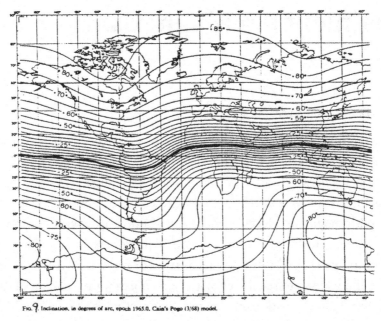

Fig. 9. Inclination, in degrees of arc, epoch 1965.0. Cain's Pogo (3/68) model.

Patterns of earth's magnetism

is usually zero, as shown in the chart. Also, the force of deflection of the needle varies from place to place, greatest in the polar regions. The strength of the force applied is evidenced in the frequency of oscillation of the inclination needle. If the force is stronger, the needle oscillates faster to and fro before it remains pointing steadily downward. All commercially obtainable magnets come with the south end of the needle weighted, to maintain it horizontal against this inclination force. They only function well in a territory for whose inclination value they were balanced. The border of a good compass rose may show the values for this deflection for the current years.

In connection with this topic, the students will often ask about the gyro-compass. This was discovered after 1900, as people tried to push the limits of exploration into the Arctic seas by submarine. A magnetic compass becomes very unclear in the polar regions—as we have indicated (especially near the poles). The magnetic compass, within the metal pressure hull of the submarine, is unusable; the thick metal hull screens it off from the earth's field, so the compass will not orient itself in a particular direction. Nevertheless, magnetic compasses are often mounted on the superstructure, with a mirror so they can be seen from below on the bridge. These are used for cross-checking for accuracy because the gyro-compass—although accurate—can easily get disturbed since the high-speed gyro is powered by an electric motor.

Experiments in Magnetism

MAG 1 FLOATING MAGNETS

Float a circular bowl, as light as possible (e.g., a plant saucer or similar plastic dish) in a large pan of water. In the dish place a magnetic body, e.g., magnetite, lodestone, or if necessary, a bar magnet. The water must remain calm (fill it the evening before) and the "raft" should float directly in the middle to avoid touching the dish. With magnetite pieces we have tested previously with a compass needle, we note where on the fragment the magnetic field comes out, and lay it in the dish on the appropriate side. This testing substitutes for repeatedly reorienting the stone in the dish and waiting to see if it clearly points north for placement on that side of the fragment. A north mark from the previous testing is utilized, and we insert it pointing eastward. If we turn the dish to the west, it will return to the north.

MAG 2 MAGNETIZING

Hammer a steel rod, about 40cm by 1.5cm (16" x ½") thick (concrete reinforcing rod) over its entire length on an inclined anvil. It must be maintained in a position which the compass shows; especially pointing downward as the inclination compass indicates. We can say to ourselves—and to the students— that of all horizontal, vertical or diagonal placements, this one produces the best magnetization. Then suspend the bar with non-twined cord (for example, fishing line), and hang a non-hammered rod a few yards away. The first pendulates about the north, the other just swings around repeatedly after a light push, and then returns to its preferred direction—but not the north. If we hold the magnetized rod horizontally in the east-west direction and hammer it there, it becomes practically non-magnetic; i.e., no longer lengthwise but diagonally magnetized, and that produces too little directional force at the ends.

MAG 3 DE-MAGNETIZING

Prior to the experiment, magnetize two long pieces of metal (e.g., steel knitting needles) by stroking them with a commercial permanent magnet. At the beginning of the experiment, we have suspended them as the earlier ones, so that the students see the magnetization. Now, heat one of them in the tight flame of several Fisher burners, until it reaches red heat. If necessary, heat the entire rod piecemeal to red heat, so that it becomes de-magnetized, as we can show after cooling it. It pendulates differently than before, and differently from the other untreated one.

MAG 4 COMPASS

Demonstrate various openly suspended compass needles from science supply houses, next to a nautical compass, e.g., an alcohol-water suspended ship's compass. Show the needle weight on the south end, the agate or corundum bearing, which is needed to prevent gradual wear from the needle point making a dent in the support. Otherwise the needle would stop moving only near the north, where the force is less, preventing the compass from showing north accurately.

MAG 5 INCLINOMETER

Hold a commercial inclinometer in a horizontal position like a compass: It shows north-seeking. Then vertically, it exhibits a minute diagonal deviation from the vertical. Thus we demonstrate the true magnetic direction in our locality of the earth (in North America, about 65° from the horizontal).

Endnotes

OVERVIEW

1   See also the various writings of Michael Polanyi on the theory of science.

2   M. Wagenschein, "Rettet die Phänomene" ["Save the Phenomena"], in *Der mathematische und naturwissen-schaftliche Unterricht* [Math & Science Teaching], Vol. 30, 1977, pp. 29–137.

3   Rudolf Steiner, *Erziehungskunst - Seminarbesprechungen* [Art of Education – Seminar Discussion] *Three curriculum lectures,* Lecture 2, Stuttgart Sept. 1919. Numbering by the author.

ACOUSTICS

1   See also interesting articles by C.M. Hutchins in *Scientific American,* 1962, 1981, on the acoustics of violins. – transl.

2   A four-piece set of resonance-figure plates as well as simple Chladni plates have been developed by Waldorf Publications.

OPTICS

1   An epistemological discussion from the mathematical viewpoint (Vol. 3) and from the phenomenological viewpoint (Vol. 2) is presented in: Georg Unger, *On Forming Physical Concepts,* Verlag Freiesgeistesleben, Stuttgart, 1967

2   Anthroposophic Press, Stuttgart, 1977, New York, 1985

3   Such a sunrise field trip makes an excellent tie-in to the introductory astronomy block, also in the 6th grade.

4   M. Stadler et. al., *Psychology of Perception,* Juventa Publ., Munich 1975, pp. 153.

5   This is worked out in a similar fashion by Hermann Buner, *Erziehungskunst,* 32, Volumes 10, 11 (1968).

6   G. Maier, *Light and the Pictorial Experience of the World,* in *Toward a Phenomenology of the Etheric World,* New York: Anthroposophic Press, 1977, 1985. Also: J.W. von Goethe, *Introduction to Color-Theory,* De la Chambre, *A History of Color Theory*; Georg Unger, *On Forming Physics Concepts,* VFG, 1961; Frits Julius, *Light-Science,* VFG, 1979.

7   For this, there are reading selections for the students; e.g., in his novel, *Rock-Crystal*, the author constantly and carefully goes into the transformations of light visible in the course of the year about the mountain. G. Blattmann, in *The Sun, Stars, and the Godhead,* strives for a new conception of the sun (Verlag Urachhaus 1972); the central idea is appropriate though most of the scientific passages are inconsequential (not too

"scientific"). Very beautiful passages can be excerpted from the book by Fynn (Sydney Hopkins), *Mister God, This Is Anna* (HarperCollins, 2005).

8   Rudolf Steiner, *The Light Course,* GA 320, Lecture VI, pp 9ff.

9   An outstanding subject teacher writes about this. Martin Wagenschein, "Save the Phenomena: The Primacy of Unmediated Experience," *Erinnerungen für Morgen* (Weinheim: Beltz, 1983, pp. 135–153). Translation by Jan Kees Saltet and Craig Holdrege, © 2008 The Nature Institute. The complete essay is at: http://natureinstitute. org/txt/mw/save_phenomena_full. htm.

10 Rudolf Steiner, *Philosophy of Freedom,* Hudson, NY: Anthroposophic Press, 1894, 1986.

11 Rudolf Steiner, *Introduction to Goethe's Scientific Works,* GA 1, 1899.

12 Rudolf Steiner, *Study of Man,* GA293, Lecture 5.

13 Goethe, *Faust.*

14 If the cord is not completely taut and droops a bit, it is not essential for building up the concept. The idea of "aligned" doesn't come out of perception, but out of "intuitive cognition." (see *Philosophy of Freedom*) Perception has the task to provide only a possibility for the soul to bestir itself in the here and now with the concept, and thereby to seek for something further.

HEAT

1   *Erziehungskunst,* 44:1,1980. See also "VII. To the Teacher" in this book.

2   With a 10-hour lag in time.

3   With a two-week delay.

4   At a depth greater than a few meters, the annual variation is less than 1 degree.

5   Rudolf Steiner, Second Natural Science course, "Warmth at the Boundary of Positive and Negative Materiality," GA321, Stuttgart 1920, New York, 1981.

6   R. Steiner, First Natural Science course; "Light, Color, Sound, Mass, Electricity, Magnetism," GA 320, Stuttgart 1919, London 1949.

ELECTRICITY

1   Amber, in old English, *lamber,* from French, *l'ambre,* like a tongue of fire, in German is *Bernstein,* literally burnable-stone. According to Roman accounts, it would be heated out of the then-gigantic deposits, that is, melted out of the mine tailings.

2   This attractive tension arises as the result of the separation we produce. Note already how electricity is connected with the will.

3   The usual van de Graaff type of generator is not the best; its inner construction is not very visible, and the belt is usually driven by an electric motor powered from a wall socket. This makes the generation of charge confusing at best. The older Wimshurst-type machine is better.

4   Some current writers refer to
    the modem approach to nature
    as "instrumental": nature as an
    instrument to express my wishes,
    only valuable if it is a tool for
    something. Contrast to this the
    earlier "sacramental" orientation
    exhibited, for example, by the Native
    American peoples: Things are sacred
    and have value for their own sake,
    for what they are, not merely for
    their utility to us.